ANECDOTAGE

Some Authentic Retrievals

★ ★ ★

Thomas L. Hughes

Fr Connie & Harld
Fondly
Tom

March 2014

Table of Contents

II – KENNEDY'S WHITE HOUSE YEARS 1961-63

IV – IN LONDON WITH ANNENBERG   125

VI – DIPLOMATS, SOLDIERS, AND BUREAUCRATS   171

VII – YOUTHFUL RETROSPECTIVES 201

IX – FROM PILGRIMS TO HOHENZOLLERNS 255

ANECDOTAGE

(Some Authentic Retrievals)
Preface by Jane Casey Hughes
★ ★ ★

"Tom Hughes would do particularly well in the new Kennedy Administration as the brilliant Director of Intelligence and Research (INR) at the State Department. Hughes was one of the few genuine intellectuals of the era, a funny, skeptical man…"
David Halberstam in "The Best and the Brightest" (1969)
★ ★ ★

The Greek origin of the word "anekdota" applies to this collection—"things unpublished." But "anecdotage" also evokes Disraeli's overtone of unreliability. (He writes in Lothair: "When a man falls into his anecdotage, it is a sign for him to retire.") Tom, although retired, hopes that these tales will not detract from his professional reputation, in and out of government.

Substantial evidence of the latter may be found in his many articles and speeches, including recent publications that provide pertinent historical context: "Perilous Encounters: the Cold War Collisions of Domestic and World Politics" (Oral history interviews with Thomas L. Hughes, published by the Association for Diplomatic Studies and Training, Xlibris, 2011). See also "Speaking Up and Speaking Out"(Xlibris, 2013).

This new collection features what Halberstam calls Tom's "funny" side— his reputation as a raconteur. As a Voice of America reporter off duty, I myself was first impressed with my future husband's story-telling talents at a lunch for interns at the Carnegie Endowment in August 1994. He had invited me, "if you have nothing better to do." He began by referring to an after-dinner speech he delivered once at St. Antony's College, Oxford. After dessert and coffee, while the port was making its rounds, the warden of the college had turned to him and said: "Are you ready to speak now, Mr. Hughes, or shall we let them enjoy themselves a little longer?" (Tom's speeches as a toastmaster at Oxford events can be read in "Oxford After Dinner," iUniverse Inc., 2011.)

What followed at the interns' lunch was a humorous whirlwind tour of fifty years of US foreign policy. During the applause, Tom stole a sly glance in my direction. This was the first of countless Washington luncheons and dinner parties over the years, where I realized that Tom's stories left those who heard him eager for more, and begging that they should be written down. A recent dinner guest thanked us for the "tasty food and memorable anecdotes (mostly supplied by the Great Anecdotist) like the one about Joe Alsop's parrot."

The stories printed here are notably different, however, from memories embellished in old age. Hence "Anecdotage: Some Authentic Retrievals." Tom was an accomplished listener, an insightful observer, and a reputable reporter—and, significantly, these situations and conversations were written up by him at the time, faithfully recording what he saw and heard.

Tom actually kept daily diaries from 1940-1960. These were his Minnesota years (Mankato and Carleton College), his Rhodes Scholar years at Oxford, succeeded by Yale Law

School, two years in the Air Force, and six years (1955-60) on Capitol Hill as Legislative Counsel to Senator Hubert Humphrey and Administrative Assistant to Congressman Chester Bowles.

While his diaries stopped in 1961 "when my life really became interesting," Tom providentially continued jotting down conversations and incidents that he found amusing. He stuffed his longhand or typewritten notes into the bottom drawers of his office desks at the State Department and the London Embassy (1961-70.) He continued this practice during the twenty years (1971-91) when he presided over the Carnegie Endowment in New York and Washington.

These written accounts have survived and provide the basis for these reprints. They are contemporary evidence of what Tom himself observed or was actually told at the time. Any embellishments of the facts (like Rusk's mistakes of timing in his account of Kennedy at Bellagio) are the original speaker's own slip-up.

Choice assignments over half a century gave Tom some unusual opportunities to experience the lighter side of famous people. Major events, no matter how serious, were also often laced with humor, even farce. Some of these stories offer rare glimpses into American presidential and political history. Others disclose delicious diplomatic and bureaucratic foibles. Many are hilarious accounts involving memorable personalities both in America and abroad. Others are merely tales of choice encounters, written up contemporaneously by Tom, and simply too amusing to lose.

The grander settings vary from the State Department to the White House, and from Capitol Hill to Embassy Row. Some of the stories are bound to be more amusing to some people than to others. Most will have a special appeal to older-generation Washington insiders who will recognize once familiar people, institutional connections, and social situations. Perhaps, however, the overall appeal may be even wider.

Many of Tom's serious speeches, inside of government and outside, were widely circulated when delivered. They usually had humorous introductions that were often reused by readers. Indeed, Tom became used to hearing his jokes appropriated later on, without attribution, by ambassadors, politicians, and even a Supreme Court justice.

Under prodding Tom has consented to this publication. I have convinced him that, as humorists go, it is better to be a has-been than a never-was. He doesn't want to refer to himself self-consciously as "Tom" or "I" in these pages. So where it is necessary to make the meaning clear, his initials "TLH" will appear.

In 1929 when he was just four years old, Tom wrote a poem called "Some Day:"

"I'm just a little beginner boy,
But I shall grow some day
Into a great big man like Dad,
Then I'll have more to say."

These recollections were originally intended for the amusement of family and friends. I hope now that a wider circle will share some of the enjoyment that Tom's many listeners have had over the years.

November 2013
Jane Casey Hughes

I

PRESIDENTIAL POLITICS
1954-60
★ ★ ★

Democratic Aspirants: The White House in View

In the 1960s, as Assistant Secretary of State in the Kennedy
and Johnson administrations, Thomas L. Hughes (hereafter
TLH) would work officially with these two Presidents. He
had already encountered them, and their rivals, at close range
in their pre-Presidential years. Indeed in the 1950s, TLH
was well positioned to watch the budding candidacies of
five would-be Democratic presidents–Kennedy, Johnson,
Stevenson, Humphrey, and Bowles. He worked directly for two
of them– twice for Senator Hubert H. Humphrey (1951 and
1955-9) and twice for Governor-and- Congressman Chester
Bowles (1954-5 and 1959-61.)

In addition to Stevenson's persistent candidacies, the 1950s
was a time of incipient and actual rivalry between LBJ and
JFK and between JFK and HHH. It was Johnson's heyday as
Senate Majority Leader. His working partnership flourished
with Humphrey, his chosen link to the liberals. It was also
a time of close personal and political friendship between

Humphrey and Bowles, as well as a growing collaboration of convenience between the two New Englanders, Bowles and Kennedy.

Presidents in Waiting

By 1956 Humphrey, Kennedy, and Johnson were all considered serious candidates for the 1960 Presidential nomination. Bowles thought of himself, and others thought of Bowles, as a dark horse in case the front- runners should fail. He soon found himself caught in the crosscurrents of the campaigns of the front-runners. He had been head of the Office of Price Administration during World War II. Later he became governor of Connecticut and a celebrated US ambassador to India. In 1959 he was a newly- elected Congressman with a national reputation of his own as a leading Democratic spokesman on foreign policy.

Alternating between Minnesota and Connecticut officeholders gave TLH early insights into the contrasting politics of the upper Midwest and New England, the rise of the Kennedy juggernaut, and the complicated political jockeying as the 1960 election approached.

Family Preliminaries: A House Divided

TLH's paternal grandfather, attorney Thomas Hughes, was a lifelong Republican and prohibitionist. Bemoaning FDR's first election in 1932, he correctly predicted that "he'll shut down the banks and open the saloons." By contrast TLH's maternal grandfather, Dr. Thomas Lowe, was a lifelong Democrat who was elected to the Minnesota state legislature late in life. So TLH grew up in bi-partisan surroundings, his parents regularly cancelling each other's votes in national elections. His mother's liberal views were bolstered by her former roommate at Carleton College, Zella Devitt, who became national president of the League of Women Voters.

Both grandfathers disliked being called "Tommy." The Welsh grandfather therefore nicknamed TLH "Tam" in honor of the Scottish grandfather. TLH went by that nickname through high school, and his oldest friends, like Walter Mondale and Harris Wofford, still use it.

By 1944 TLH was a Democrat, and at age 18 at Carleton College, he was chairman of the campus committee for FDR's fourth term. It was then that he first met Hubert Humphrey, who was busy merging Minnesota's Democratic and Farmer-Labor parties—"the only successful linkup in history of the pope, Martin Luther, and Karl Marx."

At TLH's request, Humphrey came to Carleton to speak on FDR's behalf. That meeting led Humphrey to visit Mankato, where TLH introduced him to the local leadership, including his father's Republican friends. Political meetings with Humphrey in Minneapolis soon followed.

★ ★ ★

Henry Wallace

During the 1944 campaign, both HHH and TLH were privately somewhat disappointed that FDR had dropped Vice President Henry Wallace from the ticket in favor of Harry Truman. In early 1945, TLH wrote a national prize winning oration entitled "The Century of Henry Wallace," playing off Wallace's enthusiasm for "The Century of the Common Man." The emphasis was on Wallace's domestic positions, not on his foreign policy stance.

Humphrey wrote TLH a lengthy letter dated April 12, 1945, before he knew that President Roosevelt would die that very day. Hubert was still a would-be politician who had not yet been elected mayor of Minneapolis. He wrote: "I have read your Wallace oration, and can well understand why it wins prizes, particularly when you are the orator. I hope you have sent a copy to Henry Wallace. I am writing to him in the very near future. I will call your manuscript to his attention and will also inform him of your activities out here in Minnesota.

"You have already gained quite a reputation for being a sound thinker and a capable speaker. All of us recognize your leadership ability, and are looking forward to the day when your voice will be heard in this state. We need young men who are liberals and have a firm grasp of the facts, as well as the right philosophy. Keep up the good work. There is plenty of opportunity in this country for people of your ability. I consider it a real privilege to know you, and I trust we will see each other as often as possible. The best of luck to you. Hubert H. Humphrey."

The Wallace oration led to an invitation to TLH for a private lunch with then Secretary Wallace in his office at the Commerce Department in Washington in August, 1945. When the two of them talked, they did not know that, on Truman's orders, the atomic bomb would be dropped within hours on Hiroshima. TLH wondered whether, if FDR had died a year earlier, a President Wallace would have made the same decision.

Keeping Bi-Partisan Connections

TLH was also the national president of Student Federalists in 1944, working for "world government" after the war. In this capacity he had spoken before the platform committees at both national political conventions that year. He also became friendly with Minnesota's Republican Presidential candidate, Governor Harold Stassen, and with Warren Burger, then Stassen's campaign manager and later Chief Justice of the US Supreme Court. It was a time when both major parties in Minnesota were invigorated by strong young leadership.

As SF president TLH attended the founding conference of the United Nations at San Francisco in May-June, 1945. Stassen was a delegate, already attracting national attention for the US presidency. His assistant was war veteran Cord Meyer, soon to become president of SF's parent group, United World Federalists. Cord was already married to Mary Pinchot Meyer, who years later had an affair in the White House with President Kennedy. Jack Kennedy himself, age 27, was also on the scene in San Francisco in 1945, covering the UN conference as a Hearst reporter.

Decades later there is a certain irony in the implausible bipartisan envelopments that physical structures now exhibit. Some of them innocently play post-mortem havoc with the legacies of political leaders. Thus at the University of Minnesota the Hubert H. Humphrey building wraps itself around a Harold Stassen memorial section, while in Washington the Ronald Reagan complex on Pennsylvania Avenue surrounds the Woodrow Wilson International Center for Scholars.

On the Eisenhower Campaign Train

During the summer of 1952, after graduating from Yale Law School and hearing Stevenson's acceptance speech while attending the Democratic convention in Chicago, TLH worked on the ensuing campaign. He happened to be visiting Carleton College again the day that Eisenhower stopped for a rally in the college stadium. Steve Benedict, an old SF friend who was now working for Ike, asked TLH to join the campaign train for the short trip to the Twin Cities.

TLH temporarily removed his Stevenson button. Once aboard, and without disclosing his Democratic political affiliations, Steve took him in to meet Ike and Mamie. After some small talk, Mamie said: "It was nice of Steve to introduce you, Tom. I certainly hope the youth of America will agree with you." TLH said he hoped so too.

Roger Kennedy: an Election Casualty

The 1952 Eisenhower ticket in Minnesota included TLH's Yale Law School classmate, Roger Kennedy of St Paul (later the director of the American History Museum in Washington). Roger decided to run for Congress as a Republican against Eugene McCarthy. Roger undoubtedly thought that the Kennedy name might mislead the staunch Catholic voters of Minnesota's fourth district into thinking that Roger was one of them. Helped as well by Eisenhower's popularity, Kennedy's poll ratings steadily rose.

Shortly before election day, however, the McCarthy campaign was informed that if they sent a photographer to the

House of Hope Presbyterian Church the following Sunday morning, they could probably catch Roger Kennedy emerging from the service. The fateful picture was taken and published, and Roger quickly went down to defeat. Within a few years Roger decided that he was a Democrat after all—so much so that President Clinton appointed him director of the National Park Service where he occasionally emerged as Smoky the Bear.

★ ★ ★

Soldiering Among the Slot Machines

Flying into Las Vegas to join the Air Force in October, 1952, TLH entered a huge room at the airport that had a long row of glittering slot machines. There, gambling alone, was silver-haired Senator Pat McCarran of notorious McCarran Immigration Law fame. He was busy stuffing silver dollars into a slot machine. With youthful derring-do, TLH approached him saying: "Why Senator McCarran! What are you doing here with only a few days left in the campaign?" "The campaign? Stevenson? Shit!" said the Democrat-in-name-only as he plunged in another silver dollar and pulled the lever.

★ ★ ★

Cousin Mary visits Vegas

Presumptiveness and informality were not unknown among TLH's extended family. His mother's cousin, Mary Moore Allen, had often represented one attitudinal pole among the two dozen relatives who assembled annually for Thanksgiving in Minnesota. The opposite pole was represented by straight-laced Uncle Duncan, who liked to pontificate. Once assembled, Mary would say: " Let's get the Doxology over with quickly, Duncan, so we can finish the turkey and get on with the bridge."

In her widowhood, cousin Mary moved to Los Angeles. Word reached her that TLH was now in Las Vegas. She immediately called the commander at Nellis Air Force Base asking him to transfer the call to Lieutenant Hughes. She announced her imminent arrival for a visit to TLH and the slot machines.

After official daytime duties at Nellis, TLH sampled the joys of the Las Vegas strip. Eventually this included watching Ronald Reagan on stage with the Adorabelles. An alternative attraction to sampling Las Vegas night life was to take in a nuclear explosion on the test range north of town. ("You might want to bring your dark glasses.")

Ronald Reagan: the First Sighting

In early 1981 after Reagan became president, TLH found himself at a White House breakfast. People with nametags were wandering around the East Room. TLH's tag read "Tom Hughes, President of the Carnegie Endowment." Reagan's read "Ronald Reagan, President." He sauntered up saying, "Tom, it's been so long." Skipping over some intermediate sightings, TLH said "Mr. President, the first time I saw you was 1952 when you and the Adorabelles were on the stage in Las Vegas. It happens that I've just been to communist Cuba. You might want to know that the costumes worn by the Adorabelles are still flouncing away at the Tropicana night club in Havana. Castro tells all the visitors about you and the Adorabelles."

Once One of Us?

TLH recalled, but was too discreet to mention, an even earlier Reagan. In 1948 Americans for Democratic Action had emerged as the national liberal organization of the non-Communist left. During the election that year, its monthly newspaper carried a front-page headline: "Today's ADA Leadership." Underneath were photos of Leon Keyserling. Hubert Humphrey, Chester Bowles, and Ronald Reagan. The future Republican president came to Minnesota that year campaigning for Truman and Humphrey.

Democrats for Eisenhower

In 1948 there was another prospective president, Dwight D. Eisenhower, whose political affiliation was as yet undetermined. Chester Bowles was running for governor of Connecticut, and he, like Hubert Humphrey, was part of the abortive effort by ADA liberals to induce Ike to accept the Democratic nomination for President and replace Harry Truman on the ticket.

Dewey, Truman, and Bowles

Even after the 1948 Dewey-Truman race began in earnest, efforts to glean support across party lines continued. Some well-meaning friends of Bowles took out ads in Connecticut papers with the slogan "How You Can Vote for Dewey and Bowles."

When newly elected Governor Bowles visited newly elected President Truman at the White House after their mutual victories in 1948, the President made it clear where matters stood between them by opening his desk drawer and taking out a copy of the Hartford Courant with the dreaded Dewey-Bowles headline. Nevertheless, Bowles was sent to India by Truman as ambassador in 1951, probably because the president didn't care all that much who represented him in Delhi.

Introduced to Texas

In 1953-4 TLH was on active duty at Randolph Air Force Base in San Antonio, Texas. Unmarried Air Force officers arriving at Randolph were automatically added to the San Antonio social list. Before long TLH found himself seated opposite Joan Crawford at dinner. Their conversation about Hollywood was soon interrupted, however, by two children of the hostess who were begging Mommy to let them have Jason for the weekend. Jason piloted the family airplane. "I'm sorry, darlings, but Daddy and I need Jason this weekend. He's taking us to New Orleans, where we're staying at the Courtyard of the Two Sisters. Maybe next week Jason could take you to Nassau or some other place that you'd like."

The Colonel and the Colonel's Wife

Nor was Air Force duty in Texas limited to daytime work and nighttime dinners. The Colonel kept a stable of horses, and Air Force officers were encouraged to come down from the wild blue yonder to ride them. The Colonel's wife was a determined thespian, who organized plays in San Antonio at the then new Arneson River Theater, with its stage on one side of the river and the audience on the other. Bit parts were assigned to TLH and other officers. They promptly accepted their roles as stage props in the interest of good official efficiency reports.

Seven Flags and "Translated" Speakers

There was international outreach in San Antonio as well. A prominent ladies organization sponsored an elaborate annual dinner to celebrate Texas history and to honor the "Seven Flags of Texas." The British ambassador to Washington, Sir Roger Makins, had recently addressed the meeting. After thanking him, the mistress of ceremonies had proceeded to the business part of the agenda. "Ladies and Gentlemen, I have very good news for you. We have reached our target of three hundred members. As a result, in the future we will be able to afford a much better class of speaker."

Time passed. Sir Roger Makins had in the meantime been "translated," as the British would say, into Lord Sherfield.

Unaccustomed to such renaming patterns, the San Antonio ladies now invited Lord Sherfield to address their banquet. The introducer mentioned that they would all remember the visit of an earlier British ambasssador, Sir Roger Makins. Sherfield rose to the occasion with "Same man. Same speech."

But Texans were not alone in failing to keep up with English title changes. In London when Reginald Edward Manningham-Buller, MacMillan's Attorney General, became Lord High Chancellor, he took the name Viscount Dilhorne. He soon received a letter from a Tory MP which read: "Dear Dilhorne: Allow me to congratulate you most heartily on your elevation to Lord Chancellor. Some of us were damn worried that Manningham-Buller would get it. Yours ever…"

LBJ: Another First Sighting

While TLH was serving in Texas in the fall of 1953, the Senate Minority Leader, Lyndon Johnson, was busy nearly full time in the state, starting early on his 1954 reelection campaign. Washington was still consumed with Joe McCarthy's campaign against "twenty years of treason," but "Landslide Lyndon" was determined that his margin of victory the next year in Texas would be an enormous improvement over the 87-vote margin he claimed in 1948.

Johnson had already chosen Hubert Humphrey as his conduit to the Senate's Democratic liberals. On a week's leave from the Air Force that fall, TLH had resumed contact with Humphrey at the Minnesota State Fair, and, as he watched electioneering at close range, TLH had quickly concluded that actually running for office was something he would never do. An indirect association with politics would suffice.

The Finletter Group

Out of the Air Force in 1954, TLH became assistant to Chester Bowles in Connecticut. Something called the Finletter Group had been organized at the Bowles house a year earlier. With Stevenson's encouragement, it was designed as a high-level policy discussion group. It was partly funded by Thomas Finletter, whose Air Force and Marshall Plan background arguably made him also a candidate for higher office. Meeting monthly, the group included major Democratic foreign policy figures like Dean Acheson, Paul Nitze, George Kennan, and Chester Bowles, whose rivalry was thinly disguised. Stevenson himself attended occasionally, as did Arthur Schlesinger Jr.

That summer Bowles took TLH with him to a Finletter Group meeting. Kennan surprisingly announced that he was going to run for Congress in Pennsylvania where he had a farm. This unlikely move from the anti-political Kennan evoked great mirth from Acheson and Nitze. "You? A Congressman? Tell us all about it, George." "Well, of course, I have made it clear that I will only run if I have no opposition." This prompted another outburst of laughter from Acheson and Nitze. Since opposition soon materialized, the Kennan candidacy quickly subsided.

With Bowles in Connecticut

The Bowles estate in Essex, Connecticut, regularly drew a host of celebrity visitors. Adlai Stevenson, who had been at Choate with Chet, was one. Other Democratic notables included Eleanor Roosevelt. These visits led in turn to all kinds of early connections for TLH. Bowles and his wife "Steb" were generous hosts. There was a well attended annual Memorial Day weekend for alumni of the Office of Price Administration –people who had worked for Bowles in that wartime agency. Richard Nixon was one of the few OPA veterans who failed to come.

One day Adlai Stevenson showed up at Essex, fresh from meeting with Mayor Dick Lee of New Haven. The purpose of their visit had been to discuss slum clearance. The patrician Stevenson said that his visit had been very productive, "but I kept wondering what branch of the Lee family he was from."

More exotic foreign visitors occasionally put a strain on the staff. Faith and Harry, the Irish couple in the kitchen, had particular trouble adjusting to the life styles of certain Indian visitors. When one distinguished statesman came from Delhi and word reached the kitchen that he drank his own urine, Faith put her foot down: "Well, if that's true he can do it on his own. I am not participating."

A 1954 Connecticut Election

In 1954 Bowles was increasingly devoting himself to foreign policy issues. Consequently he made a difficult decision not to run for governor again, thereby opening the door for Abe Ribicoff. TLH's new girlfriend, Jean Hurlburt Reiman, filed for the legislature as a Democrat in her largely Republican district of Orange. While losing, she ran ahead of Ribicoff in her district, and probably helped him win his narrow statewide victory.

★ ★ ★

A 1955 Connecticut Wedding

Friends from Vassar, Oxford, and Yale came to the Hughes-Reiman wedding. Chet and Steb Bowles gave the bridal dinner at Essex. The ceremony itself was held on May 7, 1955, at Dwight Chapel on the old campus at Yale. Chester Bowles was best man.

★ ★ ★

Glimpsing a Rockefeller Lifestyle

TLH used to fly to Maine in the summer months to take draft articles to Bowles at Northeast Harbor. (Ironically, the boat that Bowles rented there was "The Sea Witch," owned by Richard Bissell, later the CIA's planner of the 1961 Bay of Pigs. Opposition to that fiasco would later cost Bowles his position as Undersecretary of State.)

On one such visit to Maine Bowles asked how TLH was getting back to Washington and suggested that there was a better way than flying Northeast Airlines. A phone call to David Rockefeller, a Northeast Harbor neighbor, quickly produced an invitation for TLH to fly down to DC in the Rockefeller plane. The family conversation en route concentrated on the view from Peggy Rockefeller's plate glass window. Something was being built, say two miles out, threatening to obscure her view of the ocean. Peggy put David in charge of seeing to it that this threatened obstruction would never materialize. By the time they landed at National Airport, TLH was confident that there would be no problem.

★ ★ ★

David Rockefeller Reappears

At significant moments in TLH's career, David Rockefeller would suddenly reappear. In 1971 when TLH was about to leave government service, David came to Washington to sound him out about becoming editor of Foreign Affairs. It was a flattering offer, but TLH said he did not want to move to New York.

"Oh, if you are really unavailable, we will probably have to go for Bill Bundy. Of course, some people like Hamilton Fish Armstrong, the retiring editor, are opposed to Bill, because he was in charge of Vietnam in the State Department. But I cannot understand their qualms. After all, he's Harvey Bundy's boy, and I've known the family for years." Bill Bundy's appointment was announced the following week.

★ ★ ★

Assignment: MacArthur

At one point in Stevenson's 1956 campaign, word reached his headquarters that General Douglas MacArthur was so disaffected from President Eisenhower that the aging icon might even endorse the Democratic ticket. Bowles was dispatched to MacArthur's penthouse suite at the Waldorf-Astoria to sound the general out. TLH was already working for Humphrey, but Bowles asked him to join him in the visit.

MacArthur's disaffection was clear enough. "That man Eisenhower is just incompetent. Always has been. Knew him well. He was with me in the Philippines. Always playing bridge. Still doing it. What a disaster!"

"Well, General, if you feel that strongly, would you consider endorsing Governor Stevenson in the campaign?" "Stevenson? Oh, Hell no! That would be worse than disaster! Be serious, Mr. Bowles." With that, General Willoughby, MacArthur's aide, ushered the Democratic emissaries out as quickly as possible. Back at street level, Bowles remembered what Eisenhower had once said about MacArthur: "He was the best actor I ever served under."

With Bowles in Congress

After the 1958 elections House Majority Leader John McCormack somehow heard that TLH was coming over from the Senate to be Administrative Assistant for the newly-elected Congressman Bowles. Exhibiting the easy assumptions that Bostonians held for ethnic links, he quickly assumed that TLH was Irish (instead of Welsh) and must be related to Bishop Hughes of Connecticut. So, because of the assumed Irish connection, the Bowles office mistakenly became the beneficiary of one of McCormack's prized, and few remaining, horsehair couches. It was an honor usually reserved for those with seniority and perhaps never previously bestowed on a freshman Congressman.

Small Change

As Bowles accumulated IOUs on Capitol Hill, Fishbait Miller, then the House "Sergeant at Arms," also took the new Congressman under his wing. He advised Bowles to use his franking privilege for everything, explaining how he could then cash in his postage stamp allowance.

Rayburn and Bailey Clear the Way

In his courtesy call on Speaker Rayburn, Bowles was told by Mr. Sam how he had cleared the way for Bowles to join the House Foreign Affairs Committee, even though he lacked seniority. "I was approached by one of your Connecticut colleagues —I can't remember his name—" (actually Rep. Don Irwin) "who had the temerity to seek an appointment to that committee because he spoke Spanish. I was pleased to inform him that that place was being reserved for Connecticut's distinguished senior statesman, Chester Bowles, and that he should know better than to try to upstage such a worthy gentleman. So that's that."

The next day Bowles had a similar phone call from John Bailey, then Democratic state chairman in Hartford and soon to be Democratic National Chairman under Kennedy. He reported that Connecticut Congressman-at-Large Kowalski, the occupant of the "Polish seat" on the state delegation, had also sought a berth on the Foreign Affairs Committee "as a matter of right." Bailey reported: "I am glad to tell you, Chct, that after my little talk with him, the ambitions of your Polish colleague have ceased to exist."

A Visit to Tito

In a European trip for his new committee, Bowles took TLH along to Yugoslavia to visit Tito. Bowles was prepared to admire Tito as a non-aligned leader like Nehru, but the visit was a bit unsettling. Arriving in a US Air Force plane at Pula on the Adriatic, and then transferring to a motorboat, Bowles and TLH landed at Brioni, the island where Tito took his ease. After climbing into a jeep at the dock and avoiding camels, giraffes, elephants, and other animated gifts from Tito's non-aligned friends, they reached his old Hapsburg villa. There, amid turn-of-the-century potted palms, they were greeted by Madame Broz, Tito's formidable wife.

When the great man appeared, he was wearing a baby blue uniform with medals and carrying a field marshal's baton, Indeed Tito looked a bit like Hermann Goering. Bowles's expression suggested that a quick reassessment might be taking place. TLH was given the privilege of lighting, replacing, and relighting cigarette after cigarette for Tito's silver cigarette holder, as he puffed way throughout the afternoon.

Avoiding the Great Circle Air Route

New London and its nuclear submarine base were part of Bowles' Connecticut Second District. One day in 1960 he had a letter from a gentle, elderly Quaker couple named Weatherall whose worries about their retirement years had become acute. "You are certainly the best congressman this district has ever had, and we really regret to inform you that we will be leaving soon. We worry about our vulnerability here in New London, living right on the 'great circle air route' where World War III might start any minute. After thoughtful consideration, we have decided to seek a quieter setting for our retirement years.

"We have gone to the local library and looked up safer places that still have the benefit of Anglo-Saxon law. We have chosen the Falkland Islands, a quiet place far away from this world's hostilities. We will think of you often as you continue your struggle for peace in Washington." Years later Bowles thought again of the Weatheralls. He hoped that his ex-constituents were out of the line of fire when Margaret Thatcher assumed her role as the "Boadicea of the Falklands."

★ ★ ★

Joining Humphrey

While at law school, TLH had spent the summer of 1951 in Washington. He was a Humphrey appointee on the staff of the Senate Committee on Labor and Labor-Management Relations, researching and writing a study on "State Court Injunctions in Labor-Management Disputes." Four years later, in September,1955, Max Kampelman, the legislative counsel in Humphrey's Senate office, resigned to enter private law practice, and TLH was asked to take his place. It was an auspicious time to move to Washington. Eisenhower's continuing popularity had made Democratic presidential chances for 1956 seem slim, but Ike's unexpected heart attack had suddenly thrown political speculation into turmoil.

The new job would renew his old association with Humphrey and put TLH in charge of all legislative matters in his Senate office, except agriculture. With Hubert's membership on the Foreign Relations Committee, the foreign policy responsibilities would be particularly attractive. Moreover, the association with Bowles could remain close.

★ ★ ★

Carpooling to the Senate.

Governor Barrett Lowe of Guam and Samoa had been instrumental in the restoration of Old Alexandria, Virginia. When he heard that his Hughes cousins were moving to Washington, he encouraged them to live in the old town. Harris Wofford and Abram Chayes, close friends and Bowles associates, lived nearby in Hollin Hills.

Old Alexandria was then part of the Deep South, and TLH enjoyed the services of a Confederate carpool to travel to Capitol Hill each morning. His colleagues were the administrative assistants of three reigning southern Senators—Russell, Hill, and McClellan. It was a tribute to their southern gentility that they were willing to share their transport with a wild-eyed northern liberal. To complete the ritual, we were bid a neighborly farewell each morning by a character out of Tennessee Williams, who brought her breakfast martini out to the curb of South Lee Street to wave us goodbye.

Two years later the Hughes family moved to Chevy Chase, Maryland, where there was a carpool of quite a different nature. Humphrey himself lived in Chevy Chase, and he and his next door neighbor, George McGovern, regularly picked up TLH for the trip to Capitol Hill. Occasionally the carpool would also include Eugene McCarthy, another Humphrey protégé. In1956 it was still too early for TLH to realize that he was enjoying the carpooling companionship of three future presidential candidates.

The Moral Level

In those days senatorial assistants could mingle with Senators on the Senate floor. TLH remembers Senator Ralph Flanders telling about his farewell party in Vermont when he first went to Washington. His neighbors were gathered around a hay mow in their native hamlet, and the official spokesman bid the new Senator bon voyage with the words: "As you depart from your friends and these familiar scenes, you can be confident that in moving from Springfield to Washington, you will be raising the moral level of both communities."

After Eisenhower's heart attack in Denver in September, 1955, Republican Senator Langer of North Dakota kept mumbling: "I think they should nominate me for President. I'm older than Ike, sicker than Ike, and I need the job more."

The Johnson Legends Begin

In TLH's first days as a Lyndon–watcher, episodes on and off the Senate floor were augmented by delicious reports from Humphrey about his own visits with LBJ. Johnson himself would also occasionally visit the Humphrey office and greet the staff. TLH was already working closely with LBJ's assistants, especially Harry McPherson, Gerry Siegel, Bobby Baker, and George Reedy.

Even before he became Majority Leader, stories abounded about LBJ's mythical prowess as mover and shaker. Some of them dated back to his days as a New Deal Congressman. For example, in the 1930s FDR himself had been impressed with the newly elected Representative from Texas, and he told his New York henchman, lawyer Ed Weisl, to cultivate LBJ the next time he was in Washington. Knocking on Johnson's door in Alexandria, Virginia, Weisl heard "You-all com' on in," only to find Lyndon barefoot and lying on his living room couch, with his administrative assistant, the subsequently famous John Connally, on his knees cutting Johnson's toenails.

The Cost of Anti-Colonialism

In 1957 Humphrey and TLH were sitting together at Humphrey's desk in the Senate listening to Jack Kennedy deliver his famous anti-colonial speech criticizing the French role in Algeria. It was an important signal. Kennedy was staking out an interest in the Third World which Humphrey had hitherto considered his own playpen. Hubert was also rather miffed that his glamorous competitor had half the Harvard faculty at his fingertips, available for writing speeches. After Kennedy concluded, Humphrey rose with the obligatory congratulations on Kennedy's new interest in Africa. Then Humphrey, with TLH in tow, went up to see Johnson, who had been presiding over the event.

"Well, Lyndon, what did you think of that?" asked Hubert. "Ah think," said Johnson, referring to the wife of the French Ambassador, "that Madame Alphand ain't goin' to play the zither no more for our Jack. No way!"

Checkmating Dulles

One of Lyndon Johnson's chief motivations in appointing Humphrey to the Senate Foreign Relations Committee was to assure a quick Democratic response to moves by Secretary of State Dulles. When Dulles would announce that neutralism was "immoral" or claim credit for taking the country to the "brink of war" Humphrey would quickly engage in an ad lib counter-charge on the Senate floor and promptly reap extensive newspaper coverage. When Hubert returned to his office after one of Dulles' committee appearances, TLH asked him how it had gone. "We argued about how close to the brink he should go, and I told him if he had to make mistakes, he should try to make a new one each time."

LBJ Upstages Humphrey

Deciding that Hubert was over-achieving in his Dulles-tangling assignment, LBJ decided to get into foreign affairs himself, especially on the Middle East after Suez. This fit in with Johnson's effort to cast his net beyond Texas and the South in order to emerge as a national presidential figure. LBJ was also aware of unhappiness in the Jewish community over the Eisenhower-Dulles Mideast policy, and he hoped to enhance his own standing among those he called "the folks up North."

In February, 1957, the United Nations was threatening sanctions against Israel unless it withdrew from the Gaza Strip. Seizing the opportunity, LBJ decided to make some foreign policy himself. He sent a letter to Dulles, warning him that if he did not prevent UN sanctions against Israel "with all his skill," he could forget about any Congressional resolution supporting the "Eisenhower Doctrine" for aid to Arab states. What followed was a Johnson performance, exaggerated even for him.

Before Dulles replied to LBJ's letter, it was leaked to the press. LBJ then railed against the State Department for leaking his "personal" letter. He voiced his complaint to all those around him, including Humphrey. "Why can't Dulles keep that department of his from leaking all the time?"

Dulles, assuming that there actually had been a State Department leak, was mortified, apologized profusely, and turned things upside down to find the leaker. He sent an emissary up to see Johnson with a personal message of contrition. For two hours LBJ kept the man waiting outside his locked door. Ultimately emerging to go for a massage, the Majority Leader ran into the emissary. "Can't see you today. Come back tomorrow and try again." Meanwhile, Johnson's publicized opposition to UN sanctions on Israel was scoring handsomely with the "group up north."

Eventually it turned out that the leaker was Johnson himself. A copy of his letter to Dulles was handed to Jim Rowe, Johnson's political advance man and brother-in-law of Al Friendly of the Washington Post. The smear of the State Department played successfully for two weeks. LBJ had masterminded the whole thing and won points everywhere, as intended.

Ghosts of Guatemala

Despite the Dulles-Humphrey imbroglios, relations were preserved at the staff level. Bill ("Butts") Macomber, chief assistant to John Foster Dulles at State, had originally been at CIA. Fraternal affection must have led Allen Dulles to sacrifice Macomber in favor of his older brother. Perhaps in an effort to keep relations with the Humphrey office on an even keel, Butts would occasionally invite TLH to have lunch in the Secretary's private dining room at the State Department when Dulles was away. TLH recalls the framed colored cartoons on the walls celebrating the CIA's pro-military coup against Arbenz in Guatemala, early in the Eisenhower administration— probably another gift from Allen.

Years later, in the mid-60s, TLH visited Guatemala where the military government that the Dulles brothers installed was still in power. The ambassador invited some of the leading coupists for lunch at the embassy. As the officers, weighted down with gold braid and side-arms, arrived at the entrance hall, they were asked by the embassy butler to leave their guns on the table outside the dining room. There soon seemed to be about twice as many revolvers on the table as there were guests. Asked by TLH if this ratio was about normal, the butler said he thought there were probably a few more, safely tucked away, that had accompanied their owners into the dining room.

★ ★ ★

A 100th Birthday Party

Years later, in 1988, TLH was invited to Princeton to celebrate the 100th birthday of the deceased John Foster Dulles. By then TLH was President of the Carnegie Endowment, of which Dulles had once been chairman. Eleanor, Avery, and other relics of the Dulles family were conspicuous in the front row, together with the remains of the Eisenhower cabinet. TLH found himself sitting between Attorney General Herbert Brownell and Burke Wilkinson, the former press secretary.

The printed program listed "Opening Remarks" by George Kennan. TLH whispered to Burke: "You must have your fingers crossed over this one." Burke replied: "Oh, you know, George writes these friendly, handwritten notes. He sent one to Eleanor a couple of years ago, saying that, as far as he was concerned, bygones were bygones. On the strength of that, and since he lives here in Princeton, we invited him to open the proceedings."

Kennan took the podium, obviously relishing the situation. He began by saying that never in his wildest imagination could he have foreseen himself speaking at the 100th birthday of John Foster Dulles. "Because, you see, the Secretary and I did not get to know one another very well. As soon as he took office, he called me in to tell me that the United States government had no further need for my services. Taken aback, I murmured: 'Well, you are the decider' and started to exit the premises.

"To my surprise, I was suddenly summoned back and asked to sit at his desk to discuss Soviet-American relations. I thought to myself, this is the coldest fish you've ever met. But I later learned from my friend, John Stewart Service, that I had only seen the tip of the iceberg!" After that remark, Eleanor's hearing trumpet was going through contortions, the Eisenhower cabinet veterans were looking agitated, the students in the gallery were boisterously applauding, and the audience in general was in hysterics. Recovering decorum was difficult all around.

The Johnson Treatment

It was the Senate Democratic cloakroom in the 1950s that gave TLH his first real glimpse of Johnson at work. Standing there with two telephone receivers– one at each of his enormous ears– LBJ would converse with the two phone callers, while simultaneously watching the TV screen and seeming to conduct business with various senators as well.

One day LBJ whispered to Hubert, who was chronically short of cash, that "Tommy the Cork" Corcoran, a prominent Democratic fixer in town, would be calling at Humphrey's office that afternoon with a suitcase filled with "lucre" ($100 bills).

Another day Adlai Stevenson found himself in the cloakroom huddling with LBJ and HHH. Both were good mimics and they were entertaining an audience of fellow Senators by instructing the genteel Adlai how to talk on the phone to Jake Moore, the rough-hewn Iowa labor leader.

Manipulating the Competition

Johnson enjoyed spreading stories about one Senator to another, especially if would-be Presidents were involved. He would tell Humphrey that he had just ridden over from the Senate Office Building on the little Senate railway with Stuart Symington. LBJ then demonstrated how the well groomed Missouri senator would keep his hands on his head so that his hair would stay in place during the breezy ride. "Ah wouldn't support that Sanctimonious Stu for president of anything. No sir. Ah wouldn't."

"What's Johnson up to now?" TLH would ask Humphrey when he returned to the office after a busy day on the Senate floor. "Oh, he's just taken Estes Kefauver up to the mountain top, showing him things that the devil never showed Faust."

When the 1956 Democratic Convention convened in Chicago, Humphrey believed that he had been promised the Vice Presidential nomination by Stevenson. But Kennedy and Johnson were also interested in the Vice Presidency that year. On the convention floor, TLH watched as Adlai disappointed all three by throwing the VP nomination open. LBJ was nearly apoplectic when Kefauver walked away with the prize.

LBJ Over-Manages a Change

One of Humphrey's spectacular Johnson stories concerned LBJ's management of Senator Fulbright's takeover of the chairmanship of the Senate Foreign Relations Committee. All the committee members, including Humphrey and Kennedy, were ordered to come to the committee room the morning of January 30, 1959. "No excuses." LBJ himself would preside over a transfer of the chairmanship with the resignation of Senator Theodore Francis Green and the elevation of Senator William Fulbright as his successor.

At age 92, Green had been criticized by the Providence Journal in his home state of Rhode Island. An editorial had deplored the failing hearing and eyesight of "old mumble-stumble." Rumors were rife that staff director Carl Marcy had become de facto chairman of the committee. This morning both Green and Marcy were there with the entire committee, as LBJ began his orchestration of the change. Hubert later reported on the meeting mimicking LBJ's Texas accent:

"Now Ah know that sum of you may be unaware of the dastardly attack on our beluv'ed chairman by his home-town newspaper. When I heard of it yesterday, Ah went straight to our beluv'ed chairman to assure him that the full strength of the Majority Leader's office would be behind him in his struggle against this scurrilous attack, this vendetta.

"You know, sometimes you feel you're in the presence of greatness. You see the shades of Lincoln and Washington and the glories of the past. And that's the way Ah felt in the presence of Senator Green. Then to my surprise, the Senator said that perhaps the newspaper had a point, and that he himself had been thinking it might be time to resign as chairman, not as Senator, of course. Ah was flabbergasted. Ah protested, but all in vain. It was one of the saddest days of my life. Ah assured him that there was absolutely no criticism of his actions from the committee.

"But having heard him out, Ah thought Ah had no choice other than to accept his decision. Ah'm not one to insist that a man carry a burden he does not feel he should carry. Ah thought he deserved some respite from this uncalled-for abuse. Ah felt powerless to make the chairman change his mind."

Johnson then invited "any expressions the members wished to make." Following LBJ's lead, they went around the table, everyone praising the chairman and referring to his irreplaceable leadership. Finally Senator Aiken said: "Well, having heard the sentiments of my colleagues, I move that the committee unanimously urge the chairman to reconsider." They unanimously so voted.

LBJ didn't know when to stop. "The members of this committee have said what I said, only more eloquently, and they have repeated what I said to you yesterday, more touchingly, I think." he told Green. "They voted unanimously to ask you to reconsider." Green said: "Who did?" LBJ: "The committee. Just now." Green: "I didn't know that they had." LBJ: "Just a few minutes ago. They now ask unanimously for you to reconsider." Green, tearfully: "It didn't occur to me that it would be this way."

Now thoroughly alarmed by Green's unexpected hesitation, LBJ called for a short recess to allow the chairman to retire to an adjoining room to think over the situation. "You damn well go out there with him," LBJ whispered to Carl Marcy, "and don't you dare let him change his mind."

In Green's absence, LBJ then reversed himself 180 degrees and informed the committee: "Now we all know that this embarrassing old fart is pretty far gone, and that if he is not relieved of his duties, he might not be with us for very long. Fortunately we have the ideal successor for him, our beluv'ed colleague Senator Fulbright, who is ready and waiting to take over." LBJ again asked for "any comments from the members." So they went around the table again, with each Senator solemnly renouncing his earlier sentiments and now adopting a posture totally opposite from the one that he had fervently espoused, minutes before.

Fortunately Marcy had a smile of triumph on his face when he and Green returned to the meeting. Green reaffirmed his resignation to the unanimous relief of all concerned. LBJ's heavily staged scenario was not going to be upstaged after all. His plans had nearly backfired, but once more LBJ lucked through. Out came his press release: "Few careers have been so distinguished. Senator Green's love of his country is so great that he has decided to resign the chairmanship, an action which I personally advised against."

Humphrey in the Kremlin

A few weeks before all this, Humphrey had returned from a spectacular trip to Moscow and an 8-hour interview with Nikita Khrushchev. Before leaving Washington, he had asked TLH if he could think of anything that would help him connect with the Soviet leader. Hubert knew that Khrushchev was a dedicated ideologue, impetuous, and with a crude sense of humor.

TLH remembered a story from his English past, and he told Humphrey that it might be useful. One day Prime Minister Churchill found himself in the men's room of the House of Commons along with his opposite number, the Labour Party leader, Clement Attlee, who later succeeded him. As they approached the line of urinals, Attlee moved away from Churchill who at first complained about it, but then explained. "Oh, Clem, I understand. I know you Marxists.

Every time you see an instrument of production in private hands, you want to nationalize it."

After an initial four-hour conversation with the Soviet leader in Moscow, Humphrey found himself in the same situation in the Kremlin men's room with Khrushchev and the translator. He used the Churchill-Attlee story with its Marxist subtext, and Khrushchev literally jumped up and down with joy. "Wonderful! Wonderful! Call the Armenian!" Mikoyan was summoned, and the translator had to repeat the story. "You are a clever man, Senator Humphrey. We must talk some more." So they embarked on another four hours.

At about hour six, Khrushchev took HHH in to meet the equivalents of the Joint Chiefs of Staff in the Kremlin's war room. Pointing to a large map of North America replete with bombing targets, the Soviet leader said: "Now, Senator, where did you say you are from?" "It's Minneapolis, Minnesota, right up there in the center, near the Canadian border." Reaching for a large red crayon, Khrushchev circled Minneapolis on the map and turned to face his be-medaled generals: "Now listen! From now on, Minneapolis is off limits! We will never bomb Minneapolis! Do you understand? That's an order. No bombing of Minneapolis." During the Cuban missile crisis four years later, Humphrey wondered if that restriction still applied.

★ ★ ★

Chance Encounters

The Humphrey office was perhaps the busiest on Capitol Hill and his office hours were often the longest. As the only Democratic Senator from the Upper Midwest, Hubert in effect served as Senator for Democrats in the Dakotas, Iowa, and Wisconsin as well. During the day there was a constant stream of visitors. Gloria Steinem, then working for the CIA, came into promote student attendance at the forthcoming communist world youth festival. Labor leaders like the Reuther brothers came in to burnish Hubert's labor credentials. There were speeches to prepare for B'nai Brith, for a Harvard Law Review banquet, or for a memorial service in Minnesota for the last union veteran of the Civil War.

Some nights around 10:00 p.m., Humphrey and his staff would cross the street to the Carroll Arms Hotel for a drink at the end of the day. At the opposite end of the dining room, the already censured Joe McCarthy could often be seen with his few remaining buddies, continuing his day-long drinking, and still feisty, despite the wreckage of his anti-Communist crusade.

Other nights Humphrey would invite guests for dinner at his home in Chevy Chase. Unfortunately, there were times when he forgot to inform his wife, Muriel, about them in advance. After experiencing this predicament once too often, she began to persist in playing the piano when Hubert and her unexpected guests arrived.

The Value of a Single Vote

While working for Humphrey, TLH continued to vote by absentee ballot in Minnesota. Elections for the state legislature there were "non-partisan," i.e. candidates did not file with a party designation. In one election, TLH cast his ballot and mailed it to Mankato a few days before it was due. The ballot arrived a day late, and was suddenly featured on the front page of the Mankato Free Press.

There had been a tie for the state legislature, and the poll watchers were photographed, suspiciously eyeing the unopened ballot from Washington. To complicate matters further, there was a return address on the back of the envelope. The press account said the ballot was from "none other than Thomas L. Hughes, Legislative Counsel to Senator Hubert H. Humphrey, Senate Office Building, Washington, D.C." The situation obviously violated the voter's privacy as well.

TLH was more apprehensive than anyone else, however, because he couldn't remember with certainty which "non-partisan" candidate he had voted for. Of course, the candidates themselves made their own pro-or-con assumptions about whom TLH had favored, but no one knew for sure which way to argue. Finally, with great ceremony, the Hughes ballot was opened and counted. The right man won, and TLH was greatly relieved. The story was written up in Minnesota textbooks to demonstrate the value of a single vote.

★ ★ ★

Friends of Earl Warren

In those early days of bi-partisanship, Chief Justice Earl Warren, the former Republican governor of California, was a favorite of Democratic liberals. This was especially the case after the Supreme Court decided that school segregation was illegal. Democrats like Humphrey and Bowles, who applauded the creation of the Commonwealth of Puerto Rico, also approved of Warren's opinion that this was one of the most enlightened constitutional moves in US legal history, one

laden with positive potential. When Bowles was appointed
Undersecretary of State by Kennedy in 1961, he asked to be
sworn in by Warren.

Congressman and Mrs. Joseph Casey, TLH's future parents-
in- law, also knew the Warrens well. One day in the 1950s,
their housemaid took a phone message which read: "The chief
jester and Mrs. Worn cannot come to dinner because they are
goin to Urp."

Even LBJ found Warren useful in his larger scheme
of things. In 1965 soon after the Johnson-Humphrey
inauguration, LBJ was looking for a way to make it publicly
clear that his Vice President could not even count on the
VP's traditional role of important funeral representative.
When Winston Churchill died, LBJ deliberately by-passed
Humphrey and asked Chief Justice Warren to go to the funeral
instead.

Curiously, President Eisenhower who appointed Warren, was
anything but positive about him. Years later when TLH was
President of the Carnegie Endowment, he looked through the
1947 files relating to the selection of one of his predecessors,
the notorious Alger Hiss. The Carnegie Executive committee
that unanimously chose Hiss consisted of John Foster Dulles,
chairman, Dwight D. Eisenhower (then president of Columbia
University), David Rockefeller, and John W. Davis (the
Democratic candidate for President in 1924).

Three of the leading participants in the ill-fated Hiss
episode reappeared in another important selection process

six years later. Eisenhower had been elected President of the
US. Apparently, his memory of the role-players in the Hiss
fiasco, far from being a deterrent, was subliminally suggestive.
Two of the Carnegie trustees who had joined him in selecting
Hiss were now Ike's leading choices for Chief Justice of
the Supreme Court. Ike's first offer went to the same John
W. Davis, who said no. His second offer went to the same
John Foster Dulles, who also said no. His third choice was
Earl Warren, who accepted. "Worst mistake I ever made,"
Eisenhower was later quoted as saying.

★ ★ ★

Early Glimpses of JFK.

TLH first met Jack Kennedy at the United Nations conference
at San Francisco in May, 1945. They met again at a couple of
dinner parties in Washington in the summer of 1951 when
JFK was a young Congressman and TLH was on the staff of
the Senate Labor Committee before his final year at Yale Law
School. Kennedy himself had once intended to study law at
Yale, he said, but he had quickly decided against a legal career.
"Public service was far more appealing and far more important
than practicing law," he said, and he advised TLH to make the
same choice.

After joining Senator Humphrey in 1955 as his Legislative
Counsel, TLH had frequent meetings with JFK and his staff
in the Senate Office Building. Especially friendly working
relationships developed with Ted Sorenson, Ralph Dungan,
Mike Feldman, and Fred Holborn. TLH's path would again
occasionally cross with Kennedy's when the Senator paid
political visits to Connecticut—as, for example, at the 1956

Democratic state convention at Hartford where JFK was the featured speaker,

In 1959 after TLH became Administrative Assistant to Congressman Bowles, legislative collaboration became especially active between Kennedy's Senate office and Bowles' House office on issues like the mutual security bill, trade adjustment legislation, the Development Loan fund, and aid to India. Contacts further intensified in early 1960, when Kennedy chose Bowles to be his foreign policy adviser for the campaign, and when Bowles became chairman of the Democratic Platform Committee as well.

Checkbook Politics.

But there were irritable insights too. Glimpses into the thoroughness of the incipient Kennedy Presidential campaign were reaching the Humphrey office as early as 1958-9. Already there was testimony from Minnesota of the ready availability of the Joseph P. Kennedy checkbook.

Sargent Shriver, for example, had been put in charge of the family's Midwestern campaign. Art Naftalin, a long- time Humphrey assistant and mayor of Minneapolis, reported on his visit from Shriver. Naftalin was told that his salary could be "enhanced by $10,000 or $20,000" ("please consider your family") if he would take on the responsibility of Kennedy campaign manager for the forthcoming primaries in the Upper Midwest. Naftalin said "But surely you know that I have had a long and close relationship with Humphrey." "Of course. That's why we want you" was Shriver's reply.

Eugene McCarthy sent in a report of another Shriver visit. "There must be a small Catholic college here in Minnesota, Gene, that would appreciate a donation of several thousand dollars, given jointly in the names of Eugene McCarthy and John F. Kennedy. Wouldn't that also be of political help to you? Gene, it's all possible. Just give me the go-ahead."

West Virginia and the Roosevelts

From the Bowles office, TLH watched as the Kennedy-Humphrey primary contests unfolded. Even as Bowles welcomed his own co-option into the campaign hierarchy as JFK's house liberal, Chet had made it clear that he would not campaign personally against his old friend Humphrey. In the crucial West Virginia primary, that role was assumed by Franklin D. Roosevelt Jr.

West Virginia had been staunch Roosevelt territory since the depression. For her part Eleanor Roosevelt had made no secret of her support for liberals like Stevenson, Humphrey, and Bowles. She was also outspoken in her distaste for Kennedy. "More Profile than Courage," she said, with reference to JFK's book. An important part of Bowles' assignment in the Kennedy campaign was to mollify people like Eleanor.

Her son had ambitions of his own, however. FDR Jr. agreed to endorse JFK on stationery that was mass-mailed from Hyde Park, New York, into West Virginia. Then the Roosevelt namesake showed up in person for the primary. At Bobby Kennedy's direct instigation, FDR Jr. alleged that Humphrey had been a draft dodger in World War II in contrast to Kennedy and his PT boat. (Hubert had a medical disqualification, but had repeatedly tried to enlist.) After the election was over, FDR Jr. lamely apologized to Humphrey, but the damage was done.

Last Minute Holdouts

Although the Humphrey candidacy had ended, the Kennedy nomination was not yet assured. TLH recalls a luncheon in Washington for Averell Harriman given by his associate Phil Kaiser a week before the 1960 Los Angeles convention opened. Democratic National Committeewoman India Edwards was also at the lunch, holding forth on the socially forbidden subject of Kennedy's Addison's disease. Harriman, who regularly thought of himself as a man of presidential timber, was outspokenly bitter about Joseph P. Kennedy, accusing him of unspeakable behavior in the 1929 stock market crash and, of course, of appeasing Hitler in 1939-40. "No son of that perfidious father can possibly be any good."

After lunch the group watched President Truman, who suddenly came on TV saying that Jack Kennedy was much too young and inexperienced to be president. "He has a great future ahead of him, but meanwhile we have an abundance of good candidates—Averell Harriman, Stuart Symington, Chester Bowles..." Harriman stridently agreed: "Anybody but Kennedy." Needless to say, a week later, after JFK's nomination, no one was a more fervent Kennedy supporter than Harriman. Eleanor Roosevelt, however, left the convention in a huff, and Bowles' assignment to reconcile liberals with the ticket remained urgent.

Asserting Civil Rights

At Los Angeles Kennedy himself gave little prominence to another liberal cause–civil rights. He tolerated the strong civil rights emphasis in the Bowles platform, but counterbalanced it with his selection of LBJ as his running mate. The night that the liberal platform was adopted, TLH took it to the printers. It bore no title, and TLH on his own volition simply instructed the printer to put "The Rights of Man" on the cover. Humphrey and rest of the liberals in Los Angeles were ecstatic about the Bowles platform, which they praised as the best one in the history of the Democratic Party.

The next morning JFK offered Johnson the Vice Presidency, and LBJ surprised him by accepting. By chance TLH also witnessed Bobby Kennedy's arrival at Johnson's hotel suite when he desperately tried, but failed, to convince LBJ to withdraw in order to avoid a floor fight.

The night after LBJ's nomination, TLH had dinner at Chasen's Restaurant with his two close friends who had worked with him on the platform –Harris Wofford (later Senator from Pennsylvania) and Abram Chayes (later Legal Adviser in the State Department). Gene McCarthy and Mort Sahl sat at an adjoining table. McCarthy who had nominated Stevenson in an eloquent speech a couple of days earlier, was ecstatic in his enthusiasm for Johnson. "It's a hell of a lot stronger ticket tonight than it was last night, that's for sure." Eight years later, it was McCarthy's own campaign against Johnson in the New Hampshire primary that led LBJ to retire.

Three Sets of Brothers

There was never any love lost between McCarthy and the Kennedys. The Cuba and Vietnam crises of the '60s furnished Gene with material for his artful jibes. There happened to be three sets of prominent brothers in the Kennedy years—Jack Kennedy and his brother Bobby in Washington, Fidel Castro and his brother Raul in Havana, and Ngo Dinh Diem and his brother Nhu in Saigon. As the crises deepened in Cuba and Vietnam, Gene McCarthy started referring routinely to Bobby Kennedy as "Jack's brother Raul" or "Jack's brother Nhu."

Equivocating on Civil Rights

The Kennedy brothers' ambivalence on civil rights persisted. During the 1960 campaign, Harris Wofford was Kennedy's closest advisor on civil rights. He was responsible for suggesting and promoting JFK's famous phone call of sympathy to Mrs. Martin Luther King after her husband had been jailed. In post- election assessments, that phone call was acknowledged to have been a major factor in JFK's victory. But during the campaign, there was a furious reaction from Bobby who thought that Wofford's bad advice has just lost the South.

Before JFK's call, Wofford's advice had also reached two other prominent Democrats: Chester Bowles, who quickly phoned Mrs. King, and Adlai Stevenson, who said he couldn't do it because "we've never been introduced."

The following January, after reading the final draft of Kennedy's inaugural speech, Wofford became alarmed that it dealt exclusively with world affairs. It committed us to support civil rights "around the world," but said nothing about civil rights at home, the issue that had been vital to Kennedy's victory and was about to erupt into a major domestic crisis. Wofford protested that the new President simply could not ignore the domestic aspect and, at the last minute, the three words "at home and" were inserted before "around the world" in the inaugural text to cover the omission.

★ ★ ★

Jockeying for Place

After a strenuous campaign of travel and speeches, the Bowles entourage, known by some as "the Chet set," gathered at his Connecticut home for election night. As the returns came in, Dean Eugene Rostow of Yale Law School excitedly, but prematurely, announced that it was a landslide for Kennedy. At 9 p.m. he went back to New Haven. By midnight the rest of us were aware that it would be a narrow victory.

When Bowles congratulated Kennedy by phone the following morning, Chet inquired what he could do to help in the transition. The President-elect asked him, at once, to be his liaison with the State Department. Bowles, who, in his own mind, was suddenly competing with Stevenson to become Secretary of State, promptly went to Washington to inform Secretary Herter of his new role. Bowles and Herter had first met as governors of Connecticut and Massachusetts respectively. Despite their partisan differences, they were good friends.

Herter later told Bowles that his next visitor was his relative, Paul Nitze (they married Pratt cousins). Paul had come on an identical mission, but in his case a self-initiated one. He also put himself forward as Kennedy's representative for the transition at State. "It was a bit awkward explaining to Paul that I had been officially informed that Chet Bowles would have that job and that he had just been in to discuss it. Apparently it's every man for himself on the New Frontier."

★ ★ ★

Ironies from the Golf Course.

While the Stevenson-Bowles jockeying continued, a golf game was arranged in Florida for Kennedy and Nixon. They were joined by Florida Senator Smathers and Stevenson's assistant, John Sharon, who had been personally delivering to JFK the Stevenson task force reports that contained Adlai's refined foreign policy suggestions. Sharon suddenly phoned TLH from Florida, saying that he had some news from the golf course that he would like to convey in person.

Back in Washington the next day. Sharon had an amusing tale to tell. After teeing off, Nixon said: "Now Jack, I know you stole the election from me in Illinois. But I'm not going to reopen the campaign. It wouldn't be right." Kennedy quietly absorbed that one. "But if you make a certain appointment as Secretary of State, I would regard it as such a foreign policy disaster that I would barnstorm the country against it."

"Oh," said Jack, now mildly amused. "Who has offended you that much, Dick?" "Why, Chester Bowles, of course. He is your foreign policy adviser, isn't he? Don't you read what he writes?" "Oh, Chet sends me lots of things. What has he done to antagonize you so?" "Well, there was his Foreign Affairs article last spring. He wrote that at some point in our national interest, we are going to have to recognize Red China. Now we can't have a man like that as Secretary of State." (Fast forward to President Nixon in China, a dozen years later.)

1960 State Department Appointments

When Kennedy asked the several aspirants for Secretary of State (including Stevenson, Fulbright, Bruce and Bowles) whom they would choose as Undersecretary, they all said Dean Rusk. Since JFK had always intended to be his own Secretary of State, his choice was now obvious.

For a few specialists on ancient Greece, Rusk's selection evoked memories of Miltiades, the Athenian general who flourished around 500 B.C. and who defeated the Persians at Marathon in 490 B.C. Before the battle, the Athenian generals met to elect a commander-in-chief and a second in command. When the ballots were counted, it turned out that every man had voted for himself for the first place, and that all but one had voted for Miltiades for second place.

On December 11, 1960, JFK announced his selections– Rusk for Secretary, Bowles for Undersecretary, and Stevenson for ambassador to the UN. That night Rusk came to dinner at the Bowles house in Georgetown. It was TLH's 35th birthday and he joined the two new ranking diplomats, bringing along the Bowles list of proposed new ambassadors and high level State appointees. Rusk looked over the names and found them very impressive.

Bowles then said: "But surely, Dean, you have some suggestions of your own." "Not really. There is only one man that I insist on having with us at State—my old colleague, U. Alexis Johnson. And there is one man I refuse to have." "Oh, who would that be?" "Walt Rostow. I just can't stand having him around." (But not, apparently, for ideological reasons. Within months Kennedy sent Rostow to the State Department anyway, and. ironically, as the years passed, Rusk and Rostow vied with one another as the most persistent Vietnam hawks in town.)

★ ★ ★

Sic Transit

Secretary Herter quickly provided space in the State Department for Rusk and Bowles, and they asked TLH to join them. The three men were the only pre-Inaugural New Frontiersmen in Foggy Bottom. Operating from their inconspicuous offices in the new State building, Rusk received the A-list visitors and Bowles the B-list ones. The rest saw TLH.

★ ★ ★

Courtesy Diplomatic Passports

Among several memorable episodes during the Eisenhower-Kennedy transition was an early visit to TLH by Frances Knight, the notorious long-time head of the passport office. Over the years she had gained an infamous reputation as a regular State Department link to Joe McCarthy and J. Edgar Hoover. "Mr. Hughes, I understand that you are the person I should see." "Really? Miss Knight, what can I do for you?"

"Cancel courtesy diplomatic passports. That's what. They are a scandal. Now, in between administrations, is the only time we can get rid of them. All these free loading retirees like Robert Murphy sit on boards like the President's Intelligence Advisory Board and get 40% off on their Cadillacs from Saudi Arabia or wherever, just by waving their courtesy diplomatic passports. Reductions here. Deals there. It's an outrage." "Well, I've never heard of courtesy diplomatic passports," said TLH. "What's the downside in simply abolishing them?"

"Here is the downside, Mr. Hughes." She handed over three passports. The first read: "Joseph P. Kennedy. The bearer is the father of the President of the United States." The next one read: "Rose Fitzgerald Kennedy. The bearer is the mother of the President of the United States." The third one belonged to Mrs. John F. Fitzgerald. "The bearer is the grandmother of the President of the United States." "And these are the only problems in abolishing courtesy diplomatic passports?" "Yes, just these three. I understand that all the rest of the family will have positions in the government." "Gosh, I'm sorry, Miss Knight. I'm afraid this is a problem well above my pay grade." "Oh," she said, "I had hoped we could settle it right here."

Metropolitan Club Lunch #1

Claiborne Pell, a future chairman of the Senate Foreign Relations Committee, urgently invited TLH to lunch at the Metropolitan Club. A few years earlier, TLH had met his stepmother, the last painter-on-ivory in the Hudson River Valley. She was also the publisher of the "Olive Pell Bible" ("I just took out all the begats.") Meanwhile, her husband, Herbert

Pell, sat silently under a large Panama hat at the end of their garden. In 1960 his son Claiborne was a private person, biding his time until the WASP Senate seat from Rhode Island opened up. Since TLH was working with Bowles on Kennedy's forthcoming ambassadorial appointments, presumably an ambassadorship for Claiborne was what he had in mind.

Not at all. He wanted to discuss another ambassadorship for his father, who had been FDR's minister to Portugal in 1940! "He isn't thinking of London or Paris, but, of course, it would have to better than Lisbon. Perhaps Stockholm or Rome?" "But, Claiborne, how old is your father now?" "Around 80." "You realize, of course, that the President-elect is only 43. Everyone is recalculating these days. The presidential ambitions of two-thirds of the Senate have already come to a halt. I'm afraid you will have to discuss your father with Jack himself." (Ultimately Pell Sr. remained retired.)

★ ★ ★

Some Rhodes Scholars Apply

Nicholas Katzenbach and TLH had been fellow Rhodes Scholars at Balliol College, Oxford, after the war. Although he was in Europe and played no discernable role in the Kennedy campaign, Nick decided that he was a New Frontiersman. He suddenly flew in and asked what job might be available at State. TLH said that unfortunately State's slate seemed full, but maybe he should try Justice where his friend Whizzer White was ensconced and already making recommendations. (Nick tried Justice and later became Attorney General!)

Another old friend and Rhodes Scholar at Balliol, Phil Kaiser, had a better idea than putting his foot forward

personally like Katzenbach. Instead Phil sent a pro-
Kaiser delegation from Capitol Hill– a Senator and two
Congressmen– to plead his case for an embassy. Awed by the
gravitas of their visit, TLH upgraded their visit and sent them
next door to see Bowles. Phil was soon slated for Senegal-
Mauritania.

Metropolitan Club Lunch #2

During the transition Walter Ridder, the publisher, also asked
TLH to lunch at the Metropolitan Club. He said that his
Yale classmate, Sargent Shriver, Kennedy's brother-in-law,
was "penciling me in to be ambassador to Austria." It would
fulfill a lifelong dream, and Walter was overjoyed. TLH said
it sounded terrific. What was the problem? "Marie won't go."
"Now Walter, I am neither an Austrian tourist guide nor a
marriage counselor. From what you tell me, you may have to
make a major choice– between Marie and Vienna." " Thanks
anyway, Tom. I just thought I would test your reaction."
(Ultimately Marie won.)

Not Dancing the Night Away

The night before the Kennedy inauguration, there was a huge
snowfall that handicapped attendance at inaugural events.
TLH and his wife Jean found themselves stranded in their car
in the middle of Memorial Bridge. It was an impasse. Full stop.
Gradually, others, also caught on the bridge, stopped honking
and cursing and resigned themselves to not going anywhere. A

purple vehicle from Ridgewell's caterers was stalled just ahead. Around 11 p.m. they concluded that they were not going to make it to their assigned parties either. So they opened their doors and delivered their lobster thermidors to the hungry motorists on the bridge –all in the spirit of the New Frontier.

★ ★ ★

The Kennedys, Caseys, Lodges, and Hugheses

There were actually some convoluted, but unexpected, connections between these families over the years. Three-term Congressman Joseph Casey from Massachusetts was a New Deal Democrat and protégé of Franklin Roosevelt. In 1942 FDR asked Casey to run for the Senate against Henry Cabot Lodge. Joseph P. Kennedy quickly called an emergency family meeting at Hyannisport, and the question was: "Do we really want to have a handsome, young Irish Catholic Senator from Massachusetts whose name is not Kennedy?" The emphatic answer was "No, we do not."

Grandfather Fitzgerald was speedily pressed into service to head off this calamity and run against Casey and defeat him in the Democratic primary. Unfortunately Casey won and became the nominee. Another emergency meeting at Hyannisport posed the same question and produced the same answer. This time Kennedy money supported Lodge in the final campaign and Casey lost.

Writing to his soldier son Joe Junior, Joe Senior recapitulated these events adding a warning about dating Protestant girls: "Come back and marry a good Irish girl, and your political future is limitless." He explained that Casey lost in part because he had married a Protestant and their daughter Jane was born six months after the wedding. (TLH married Jane in 1995 after the death of his first wife.)

The Congressman's wife, Constance Dudley Casey, was President of the Woman's National Democratic Club. She introduced TLH for a speech there in the 1970s, unaware that he would later marry her daughter. Meanwhile, her youngest daughter, Jane's sister Caroline, was married for a time to Reed Cosper, a cousin of TLH.

One Christmas day in the late '70s, the Cospers knocked on the Hughes front door. Caroline, a soothsayer, said: "We won't keep you long. I just asked Reed whether we knew anyone who might have some Cuban cigars. They are illegal, of course, but my father, Congressman Casey, craves them nevertheless." Caroline had no way of knowing that TLH had just been to Cuba where Castro had given him a box of cigars. "They're on top of the refrigerator. Help yourself." Jane recalls how pleased her father was with Caroline's timely present.

This was years before TLH knew any of the other Caseys. He was aware, of course, that Jack Kennedy, himself, had defeated Senator Lodge on schedule in 1952. Later, while engulfed with Vietnam at the State Department in the 1960s, TLH got to know Lodge, who, by then, was JFK's ambassador in Saigon.

To add to these interrelationships, Ambassador Lodge's son, George Lodge, and JFK's sister, Jean Kennedy Smith, overlapped for eight years in the 1980s on the board of the Carnegie Endowment for International Peace while TLH was president.

★ ★ ★

II

KENNEDY'S WHITE HOUSE YEARS
1961-63

Ike's Bequests: Laos and the Cuba Landing

President Eisenhower left two farewell presents for his successor. The first was Laos, which Ike warned was a potential catastrophe– a falling domino. The downside, Ike said, was that American troops would probably have to be sent in to save it. The upside was that we could easily capture the place, because the Lao soldiers were all homosexuals.

The planned invasion of Cuba by American-trained-and-equipped Cuban exiles was already far advanced when JFK took over. According to the Eisenhower administration planners, Allen Dulles and Richard Bissell, American involvement would be deniable and the anti-Castro Cuban populace would rise in support of the invaders. (However, if they did not, the American president would be forced to commit the US military to rescue the operation—or so the planners privately believed.)

Bowles a Casualty of the Bay of Pigs

For the first three months of the Kennedy administration, TLH remained with Bowles as his chief assistant in the Undersecretary's office. During the campaign Bowles had already been apprehensive about Kennedy's bellicose statements about Cuba, and he worried about their future effects on Cuba policy. When Bowles tried to get Dick Bissell released from the CIA to take a high level economic post at State, Chet was informed by Allen Dulles that Bissell was indispensable at the agency. He was involved in a major secret enterprise, and could not possibly be spared. Indeed Bissell was hard at work– planning the Bay of Pigs.

In late March when Bowles first learned that an invasion by the Cuban exiles was actually about to occur, he wrote a personal memo to the President opposing the entire operation. TLH collaborated in writing the memo. Not wanting to send it directly to JFK out of channels, Bowles gave it to Rusk, asking him to pass it on to the President. When, a few days later, Bowles asked Rusk if he had delivered it, Rusk said "No, actually I didn't, because nothing is going to happen." Kennedy himself never saw the Bowles memo.

When it happened after all, word got around about the memo and Bowles was caught up in the recriminations. At a White House meeting, he was acrimoniously and physically upbraided by Bobby Kennedy. The Attorney General punched Bowles in the chest, and, with the President silently observing it all, Bobby declaimed in front of the assembled group: "Let's get this straight, Chet. You supported the Bay of Pigs just like the rest of us." Following that altercation, Bowles' days as Undersecretary were numbered. He was fired a few months later, and after some time in an ill-defined job as presidential assistant for the third world, he returned to India for his second ambassadorship there.

A New Adventure on the New Frontier

Somehow TLH's long association with Bowles and his role in helping prepare the memo were not held against him, even though the facts were known at the White House. Instead TLH actually became a beneficiary of the Cuban fiasco. Later that same month, he was appointed Deputy Director of the Bureau of Intelligence and Research (INR). In the wake of State's non-involvement in CIA planning for the Bay of Pigs, INR was now assigned enhanced responsibilities in vetting CIA- proposed covert operations. In becoming deputy to an old friend, INR Director Roger Hilsman, TLH's new role was part of that post-Bay of Pigs enhancement. Inside the bureau, this new responsibility for covert vetting was compartmentalized, of course. The main responsibility of INR remained research and analysis.

Whose View of the World?

Democratic liberals had been dismayed when JFK's first appointments were announced. They were those two well-worn holdovers from the Eisenhower era—J. Edgar Hoover and Allen Dulles. TLH's friend, Harris Wofford, had campaigned for Kennedy by proclaiming that JFK shared the "Stevenson-Humphrey-Bowles view of the world," but that JFK had the added advantage of being electable. After the Hoover-Dulles retentions were announced, TLH sent a postcard to Wofford that read: "Thanks for convincing me to vote for Kennedy's "Stevenson-Humphrey-Bowles-Allen Dulles-J. Edgar Hoover view of the world."

★ ★ ★

"Please Join me in Welcoming…"

President Kennedy also took the liberty of placing Deirdre Henderson in INR. Deirdre was one of the many women left over from Kennedy's campaign. She had had a floating role as "liaison" with the academic community during the election. She continued with a kind of pleasantly roving presence in INR. TLH assumed that, if she was so minded, she would keep the White House abreast of any people, attitudes, or events she observed that might be of interest over there.

★ ★ ★

The Last Dulles at State

One of the first phone calls to TLH, after he joined INR, was from Allen Dulles, who was still CIA director. Eleanor Dulles, his sister, was in INR at the time, working on Berlin. "Tom, I know that my sister is over there in your bureau," he said, "and if this ever becomes embarrassing for you in any way, just let me know, and I will put her someplace else." It was news that he had "assigned" her to INR in the first place, back when her other brother was Secretary. Here was one more CIA practice, left over from the Dulles-Dulles days, that would now be discontinued.

Eleanor looked at Berlin with proprietary affection, and in August, 1961, she was deeply upset when the Berlin Wall went up. Accusing the Kennedy Administration of neglect, or worse, that weekend, she went after anyone she could find. Martin Hillenbrand, the Berlin desk officer, unfortunately was near at hand in the State Department, and she berated him literally all the way into the men's room.

Eleanor Dulles used to visit Communist East Germany, driving around alone in her Volkswagen. When stopped by the police for a traffic infringement, she would roll down her window, shake her umbrella at the Volkspolizei, and accost them in German: "You obviously don't know who I am. I am Eleanor Dulles. My older brother was the American Secretary of State and my younger brother was the Director of Central Intelligence." Then, rolling up her window, she would drive on. The VOPOS were apparently too startled to pursue her.

An Uncertain Start in Pakistan

Pakistan was one of few diplomatic posts left open in the list of recommended appointments that Bowles and Shriver sent to JFK. At length Rusk weighed in on behalf of Assistant Secretary Walter P. McConaughy, a Foreign Service officer whom he remembered from the 1950s. Shortly after his appointment, Jackie Kennedy decided to visit Pakistan. In briefing sessions before her trip in 1962, she was asked by the Pakistan desk officer at State to build up the new ambassador's reputation in her meeting with President Ayub.

Ambassador McConaughy joined her at the meeting. Nevertheless, in due course, Jackie began her breathless spiel.

"President Ayub. I want you to know how lucky you are to have such a close friend of President Kennedy here as our new ambassador. I can vouch for him completely. He is one of our personal favorites– one of the few who has immediate access to the White House, day or night." At that point the fledgling ambassador spoke up: "Now, Mrs. Kennedy, you mustn't continue like this. You are mistaken. Why, I've never even met your husband!"

Saved by the Swiss

Switzerland was another post that had been left vacant in the Bowles-Shriver ambassadorial recommendations. They had heard that JFK had his own choice for Bern. This turned out to be one Earl E. T. Smith, a rather unsavory Florida family friend, whose earlier connections with the pre-Castro Cuban dictator Batista were hardly a recommendation. Speculation grew that Kennedy's interest in having Mr. Smith out of the country had something to do with his own admiration for Mrs. Smith. At any rate, the Swiss ultimately refused to take Mr. Smith on the grounds that his Batista background was incompatible with their official role in handling Cuban interests for the U.S. So the Smiths were not separated, and family values won out after all.

A Presidential Rivalry Resumed

Early in the Kennedy Administration the President's old rival, Adlai Stevenson, now his new ambassador to the United

Nations, was hosting a reception at his Waldorf-Astoria residence. JFK himself was there, but off in a corner with Adlai's press man, Clayton Fritchey. Adlai was center stage surrounded by several of his adoring women—Agnes Meyer, Marietta Tree, Jane Dick, et al.

According to Fritchey, JFK surveyed this scene and said: "Just look at that balding, paunchy old has-been, surrounded by all those doting female admirers. Clayton, you know him well. What does Adlai have that I don't have?" Rising to the occasion, Fritchey replied: "Well, Mr. President, I think I would have to say that Adlai is genuinely interested in what women think about foreign affairs." "Oh, I couldn't go THAT far," Kennedy responded.

Reversing Roles at Halloween

Adlai Stevenson happened to be staying overnight in Georgetown with Bowles in 1961. It was Halloween and some neighborhood children rang the doorbell. They asked the maid whether she could produce some old Stevenson campaign pins. When she left to inquire, Adlai himself accidentally appeared at the door. The tricks-or-treats children recognized him, screamed, and fled.

This was not the first time Adlai had been spooked by Halloween. He himself was fond of recounting the visit to Chicago of the President of Guinea in 1959. Stevenson had invited Sekou Toure and his entourage for dinner. He had told Viola, the maid at Libertyville, to prepare for a dozen guests who would arrive around 6:30. Then he called back to say there would be twice that number. She had planned on beef stroganoff, and that now needed to be supplemented. Since she had some ham, she added it to the beef.

Adlai himself expected to be there ahead of time, but he was delayed in Chicago. The Guineans arrived ahead of him, all wearing their flowing native robes. Viola thought they were playing trick-or-treat. She gave them candy and peanuts, and closed the door. The State Department's lady escort then rang the doorbell and explained that they were the expected guests, not trick-or-treaters. This time Viola let them in and asked for their hats. They refused and remained fully costumed.

When Adlai arrived, Toure commented on the unusual American custom of offering guests candy and nuts at the front door. Dinner was served. Then someone asked in French whether there was ham in the main course, because Muslims can't eat pork. "No, this is beef stroganoff," Stevenson explained. Whereupon, at the other end of the table, the oblivious escort officer exclaimed: "Governor Stevenson, this ham is simply delicious."

At that point genuine trick-or-treaters rang the doorbell. It was Marshall Field and family, also dressed in billowy robes. Viola thought they were part of the diplomatic party and asked them in. Before long they were also invited to help themselves to the ample ham stroganoff left over from dinner.

★ ★ ★

State Department Briefings

For eight years, from 1961 to 1969, TLH's daily routine in Washington was to rise at 6:30 a.m. and drive to the State Department in time for INR's 7:30 a.m. staff briefings of worldwide overnight intelligence. Using that all-source material, he then privately briefed Rusk and the various Undersecretaries at 9:00 a.m.

In addition, once a week, Rusk also held a large staff meeting for the twenty top officials of the State Department. TLH began all of these sessions with a classified fifteen-minute worldwide roundup, answering questions, and performing at length across the table from luminaries like USIA Director Edward R. Murrow, Averell Harriman, the Rostow brothers, Llwellyn Thompson, Harlan Cleveland, and occasionally Adlai Stevenson and other visiting ambassadors.

Relaxing at Lake Como

Years later TLH was a speaker at Dean Rusk's 80th birthday party in Atlanta. In an expansive mood at the dinner table, Rusk turned to him and asked if he had ever told him about President Kennedy's visit to Bellagio. "I thought your recollections were all confidential and all going to your grave, Mr. Secretary." "That's true of most of them," said Rusk, "but for this exception tonight."

"President Kennedy was looking at our heavy official schedule for Europe and asked if I happened to know of a secluded spot where he could go for a quiet weekend after all our official business was over. I figured he was thinking of the Villa Serbelloni on Lake Como, since I had been president of the Rockefeller Foundation that owned it. Such a request of course, broke all the foundation's rules, but I had visions of some relaxed, informal, talks with the President about his foreign policy goals, which we had never really had a chance to discuss one-on-one." (In his account Rusk inaccurately placed the Bellagio visit as a weekend in 1961 after Vienna. Actually it was a weekday in 1963 after Berlin.)

"So I boldly phoned my successor at Rockefeller and said that President Kennedy had hinted that he might be free to spend some quiet time at the Italian villa. Perhaps this could even be considered a national security matter, since he and I had so much to discuss. The foundation patriotically agreed to vacate the villa, and the Secret Service was speedily dispatched to check out the premises.

"When the appointed day arrived, President Kennedy and I were standing on the tarmac at the airport in Milan. He turned to me and said: 'Mr. Rusk –he always called me Mr. Rusk–it was damn thoughtful of you to arrange this weekend for me at Bellagio. That villa is just what I need. I am really looking forward to relaxing there. I can't thank you enough for your trouble. Well, so long! See you back in Washington!' "With that," Rusk ruefully concluded, "the private planes started arriving, bearing his female friends. I realized then what a relaxed weekend this was going to be and for whom."

While reminiscing about his achievements as president of the Rockefeller Foundation, Rusk also disclosed that the foundation had originally funded the Kinsey report. "But, of course, when I saw what they had come up with, I quickly decided that we couldn't publish it."

High Life on the New Frontier

The Kennedys introduced a glittering social life to Washington, and the foreign embassies fully participated.

On one special occasion the Diplomatic Corps gave a white tie dinner at the Pan American Union in honor of Dean and Virginia Rusk. Lots were drawn for two escorts per person to ascend the tall staircases leading from the palms and fountains on the ground floor to the majestic dining room above. TLH's wife Jean scored in a major way that night by drawing as escorts both British Ambassador Ormsby-Gore and Soviet Ambassador Dobrynin. TLH had to content himself with the ambassadorial wives from Togo and Niger.

Come to Think of It

Lunches in the 1960s were often two martini affairs. There were official lunches at Blair House or in the State Department. Foreign embassies entertained lavishly, and the Hugheses were invited frequently by the British, German, and Indian ambassadors. There were working lunches in the White House mess with Ted Sorensen, Ralph Dungan, and Arthur Schlesinger in the Kennedy administration, and with Bill Moyers, Harry McPherson and Walter Jenkins in the Johnson days. Foreign diplomats and American journalists competed with one another to entertain at the Federal City Club, the Jockey Club, the Hay Adams, the Madison hotel, the City Tavern, the Occidental, the Golden Parrot, the Colony, Paul Young's, or French restaurants like the Pigalle, Le Bistro, Rive Gauche, Chez Francois, and La Salle du Bois.

Meeting the Press

One morning shortly after TLH moved to INR in April, 1961, Secretary Rusk called him up to his office to discuss relations with the press. There had been a leak to the Washington Post and some fingers had pointed to an informant in INR. Rusk began by saying that he himself, in moving to Washington, had quickly come to appreciate where the power lay in the nation's capital. He had barely been sworn in before he was contacted by James (Scotty) Reston and Walter Lippmann, "both of whom indicated that if I ever had a matter of importance that I wished to disclose, they would be happy to receive me."

Bearing such journalistic supremacy in mind, Rusk wanted to know why anyone in INR ever had to talk to the press. "After all, you are an internal unit here at the State Department. You are not policy makers. Why does anyone in your bureau ever have to meet with a newsman about anything? Why shouldn't we just prohibit all contacts between INR and the journalists?"

TLH replied that such a rule might be rather hard to enforce. "Why would that be?" asked Rusk. "Well, for example Mr. Secretary, I had a call about a hour ago from Joe Alsop, President Kennedy's great friend. (The papers had been full of stories about JFK's midnight visit to Alsop's house on his inauguration night.) Alsop told me today that President Kennedy had suggested that he (Joe) and I should have lunch. Now, maybe Alsop is making this up. On the other hand, maybe he isn't. So I need your considered advice, Mr. Secretary. Please tell me what you think I should do."

There was a long pause. Then Rusk reached into his right-hand desk drawer and took out a glass of Scotch that had already been poured to fortify him for the day's work. He took a swallow and replaced the glass. TLH continued: "Meeting Alsop, of course, would violate the INR press rule you were just proposing." Rusk assumed a Buddha-like pose, his usual posture when he was thinking deep thoughts. Finally he said: "Well, perhaps you had better go." That was the last time during Rusk's tenure that a prohibition on INR press contacts was broached.

The Parrot Made Three

Thereafter, TLH saw Alsop perhaps a dozen times during the Kennedy administration, usually at handsome luncheons in his Dumbarton Place dining room amid his ancient Chinese bronzes. On TLH's first visit, the third party in the room was Joe's highly intelligent parrot, who greeted visitors with the words: "Well, look who's here!"

Communist aggression was usually Joe Alsop's chief preoccupation, and he would report that his CIA sources were telling him that the Pathet Lao were threatening to take over in Laos. Did I think the communist victory was imminent? TLH would pause, wondering how Joe's friend the President would expect him to answer. The parrot would suddenly bark: "Beats me!"

The parrot's repertoire included two other bright remarks that fitted any conceivable lapse in conversation. Alsop would say: "I hear rumors in Saigon that Diem's brother Nhu is secretly in touch with Hanoi and could possibly be working out a deal behind our back." Again there would be a pause while Joe's guest savored the roast. The parrot would screech:

"Think of that! Think of That!" "You know, Tom," Joe would continue, "I even hear of coup plotting by unhappy generals in Saigon." Then the parrot would mutter "Well I never!"

Joe's parrot was the best opportunistic commentator in town. He had three suitable all-purpose answers ready to upstage whatever guest Joe was quizzing. Although the parrot's cage could be covered to silence him, before long he was nevertheless given away—probably not too soon for some of Joe's more sensitive and self-important visitors.

A Legacy from Look

Kennedy himself had to deal with journalists, not only the multitude outside, but some of his own appointees inside the administration as well. Two of his ambassadors in Africa, for instance, spent much of their time jousting with one another, just as they had previously done when both were journalists at Look Magazine. Ed Korry in Ethiopia and Bill Attwood in Guinea projected their personal rivalries into the New Frontier.

Cables from Conakry fretted about Korry's fawning over the Ethiopian emperor in Addis Ababa, while cables from Addis fretted about Attwood's inability to tilt Sekou Toure's neutralism in the Cold War. Few messages to Kennedy from either ambassador failed to warn about the other. When their warring Christmas cards reached the White House, JFK told Rusk: "I'm glad they are a continent apart. My sympathy for Gardner Cowles (Look's publisher) grows day by day."

JFK at State

President Kennedy's own press conferences were usually held in the State Department auditorium. At their conclusion, he would often go up to Rusk's 7th floor office and meet there with the State Department's top officials. In this way personal impressions began to register with him. These impressions stimulated his addiction for personal phone calls to lower levels in the bureaucracy. When JFK appointed TLH to direct INR in April 1963, he was said to be the youngest assistant secretary of State in memory.

The President occasionally hosted receptions of his own in the diplomatic rooms on State's 8th floor. There were also, of course, frequent ceremonial occasions at the White House where TLH and his colleagues were invited—like the proclamation of the Alliance for Progress or Randolph Churchill's visit to accept his father's honorary citizenship papers.

★ ★ ★

Upsetting the Pentagon

In October, 1963, using the Pentagon's own "body count" statistics from Vietnam, INR published an intelligence memo that concluded that the US was losing the war, not winning it as the Pentagon repeatedly claimed. The Joint Chiefs protested INR's right to use their statistics, and McNamara wrote to Rusk, more or less proposing that he fire TLH.

Rusk, an ex-Colonel who usually deferred to the Defense Department, summoned TLH and asked for particulars. TLH explained that INR always consulted the military on such matters, but never allowed the Pentagon to clear the final INR product. Reminding Rusk that he had always defended the autonomy of INR to reach its own conclusions, he fended off Rusk's suggestion that perhaps some military officers might be assigned to INR to help out. During the last month of the Kennedy administration, this was still an issue. Ultimately Rusk replied to McNamara assuring him that INR always "consulted" the Pentagon when interpreting military statistics.

Later Glimpses of McNamara

In the final years of the Johnson administration, the Pentagon and INR were frequently at loggerheads over Vietnam estimates. By 1967 McNamara himself had notoriously become a hawk by day and a dove by night. Once that year when TLH happened to be visiting with Ambassador David Bruce in his office in the London Embassy, the ambassador paused to take a phone call. For his part, Bruce made a few brief comments like "Oh, I see" and "I had no idea, Bob."

When the conversation was over, the ambassador said: "You can't imagine who that was. It was our Secretary of Defense. He and I tangled rather seriously at a White House meeting on Vietnam last week. He just called to tell me that what he had said at that meeting was his public position, but that privately he agreed completely with every skeptical thing that I said about the war."

In retirement McNamara and TLH became occasional associates, serving together on boards like the Arms Control Association and the Battelle Pacific Northwest National Laboratory. After writing a critical review for Foreign Policy magazine of McNamara's book "In Retrospect,"TLH sent him a courtesy advance copy saying "You won't like this." He wrote back: "You're right, but thanks for alerting me." A few days later, in advance of a Battelle board meeting, McNamara phoned TLH from somewhere in Asia (Nepal?) to suggest that Vietnam should be avoided at the forthcoming meeting. TLH reassured him that Vietnam was not on the Battelle agenda and that, as far as he knew, no one had any intention of bringing it up.

Hoover Meets the Bear

Soon after joining INR in the spring of 1961, TLH was invited to the Chevy Chase Club one night as the guest of Allen Dulles. His dinner party was in honor of German General Reinhold Gehlen, Hitler's former intelligence chief on the eastern front, who had turned his files on the Soviets over to the CIA in return for rehabilitation.

TLH found himself sitting next to J. Edgar Hoover who was increasingly mystified as Gehlen went on and on about "the bear." "What is this bear he is talking about?" Hoover asked TLH. "I think it is the Soviet Union, Mr. Hoover." "Oh, very good. VERY GOOD. I will tell my men at FBI headquarters. The Bear. Very good."

Two Security Clearances

At about this same time, confidence in Hoover's Bureau was not exactly enhanced when an FBI agent came to interview

TLH concerning the security clearances of two possible appointees in the Kennedy administration. The first was Averell Harriman and the second was Adlai Stevenson. The agent mentioned that "they certainly have strange first names," but beyond that he seemed unfamiliar with either man.

"How long have you known this person?" "Do you consider this person to be a patriotic American?" "Do you have any reason to doubt this person's loyalty to the United States?" "Would you recommend this person for a position of trust?" TLH vouched for both persons, but any smiles would definitely have been suspect. Both persons must have passed the security hurdles, however, for their appointments were soon announced.

★ ★ ★

A Complaint in the Family

Not everyone checked by the FBI in those days was so lucky. Edward Sterling Hughes, a cousin of TLH, also stopped by INR for a visit. "Ned" Hughes was a conservative businessman from Ann Arbor, Michigan, where he was employed in the top echelon of the Ford Motor Company. However, Ned was worried. He claimed that he was being stalked. Wherever he went, whether in Detroit, London, or Paris, someone was following him. TLH shook his head in disbelief. "Ned, you are sounding paranoid."

But cousin Ned persisted, recounting the following story. Before his appointment as Kennedy's Secretary of Defense, Robert McNamara had been the president of Ford. At a staff meeting one morning, McNamara had suggested that a hard look should be taken at the company's pro bono spending. He was wondering especially about Ford's expensive financing of the TV program, "The FBI in Peace and War." He turned to Ned and said: "Mr. Hughes, please investigate this program seriously and tell me whether Ford funding should be continued."

This glamorized series on the FBI, full of flattering episodes, was known to be one of J. Edgar Hoover's personal favorites. Nevertheless, after a probing investigation, Ned recommended that Ford's funding should cease. One can imagine Hoover's fury. Shortly after the funding stopped, the stalking started. In hindsight, given what we subsequently learned about the personality cult and idiosyncratic behavior rampant at the FBI, cousin Ned's suspicions seemed entirely plausible.

★ ★ ★

A Visit to the Director

In 1967, Evan and Allan, TLH's two sons then aged eleven and eight, decided they wanted to visit FBI headquarters and even meet the great man. The visit took some effort to arrange, but ultimately Hughes and sons were ushered into the director's office. There behind a massive desk stood J. Edgar Hoover, looking rather like Mao Tse-Tung. The boys showed him their empty cartridges, to prove that they had already visited the shooting gallery below.

Suddenly Allan discovered Hoover's display of autographed baseballs. "Where did you get these?" Allan asked. Picking one up, J. Edgar said: "Jackie Robinson gave me this one when he was with the Orioles." Allan, his eight- year- old interlocutor, countered with: "No, Jackie played with the Dodgers." "Well, be that as it may," the Director responded. "Perhaps it's time for the camera."

A cumbersome Victorian photographic contraption on wheels was then rolled in. The boys were stationed on either side of the Director who placed his hands on their shoulders. Their father was eased out of camera range. Several flash bulbs popped. Then Hoover said: "Thanks so much for stopping by." With that the three Hugheses were ushered out of the presence. The next morning two motorcycles, with sirens blaring, stopped at the Hughes home in Chevy Chase. A large package was delivered, containing colored photos of the visit to the FBI. All were autographed "To Evan and Allan from their friend, J. Edgar Hoover." No one knows quite what to do with those pictures, even now.

★ ★ ★

Clark Clifford—Outside but In.

Early in the Kennedy administration TLH also found himself in the law office of Clark Clifford, who had often served as JFK's family attorney. Clark was then a junior member of the President's Foreign Intelligence Advisory Board, which had been reactivated by JFK after the Bay of Pigs.

Clifford motioned for TLH to sit in the visitor's chair, strategically placed opposite him, across his desk. Then, slowly but dramatically, the blinds opened on the window behind him, disclosing a perfectly framed view of the Capitol dome, and clearly testifying to the importance of this lawyer-adviser in the Washington establishment.

"Tom, I want you to know that I rely upon you as my personal eyes and ears in the State Department," this prototype outsider-insider began. Even then there was no love lost between Clark Clifford and Dean Rusk. Back in the late 1940s in the Truman administration, they had been antagonists (Clifford pro and Rusk con) in the big internal administration argument over recognizing the state of Israel.

A Picnic for PFIAB

In April, 1963, the same month when he appointed TLH as head of INR, President Kennedy appointed Clifford chairman of the President's Foreign Intelligence Advisory Board (PFIAB). In due course, the heads of the various intelligence agencies were invited to Clifford's home in Bethesda to meet the other PFIAB members. After several drinks, the group gathered for supper at a picnic table on the lawn behind the residence.

Clark was entertaining the group with his repertoire of reminiscences about presidents he had known. He had just reached the apocryphal story about Eisenhower on the Burning Tree golf course, momentarily removing his hat out of respect, while in the distance Mamie's funeral procession passed by. One of the PFIAB celebrities, retired General Jimmy Doolittle of Tokyo bombing fame, was sitting at the end of the bench. Jimmy had had a considerable amount to drink, and he suddenly fell over backwards and rolled down a small hill. With allowance for their varying agilities, the combined forces of PFIAB and the intelligence community scrambled to the rescue.

At evening's end, Pat Coyne, PFIAB's ubiquitous secretary, was informed by his new chairman that the Doolittle incident need not be recorded in the official minutes of the occasion. Knowledge would be restricted to those who had a need to know—in this case, only those present.

Clark Clifford Extended.

Clifford and TLH remained collaborators during Clifford's tenure as Secretary of Defense, when he was instrumental in winding down the Vietnam War. They remained friends after both left government. Years later when Governor Cuomo was thinking of a presidential run, TLH was commuting to his Carnegie office in New York and found himself sitting next to Clifford on the Eastern shuttle. TLH asked him how he reacted to a possible Cuomo candidacy.

Clifford drummed his fingers typically and replied: "Well, you know, I have been introduced to Governor Cuomo perhaps a dozen times. Each time it is a new experience for the governor. Of course, Tom, I'm from Missouri. Out in Missouri, there are very few men named Mario and almost no one named Cuomo."

The super-lawyer from Missouri went on to say that he had recently been entertained by the fugitive Robert Vesco on his private aircraft. Vesco had tried to impress Clifford with his elaborate lifestyle, out of legal reach in Central America. After much solicitous conversation, Vesco asked whether Clifford would agree to represent him in Washington. Clark replied: "Mr. Vesco, you don't need a new lawyer. You need a new story."

Christmas at USIB

In the Kennedy years, the high degrees of classification for codeword intelligence were marked by their distinctive red or black covers when carried by their couriers around Washington. At one pre-Christmas meeting of the US Intelligence Board, a group of the CIA's advent choristers, led by John McCone himself, burst into the room lustily singing "Oh Come All Ye Faithful" and "We Three Kings of Orient Are." The words and music for the Christmas carols were hidden inside the same red and black covers that the spies used on their daily briefing rounds.

The Cuba Missile Crisis

The high point of the Kennedy administration was, of course, the Cuba missile crisis. The world came the closest it has ever come to nuclear war. Once the crisis reached fever pitch, President Kennedy rose to the occasion and performed optimally, in spite of his own prior hawkish posturing and the strident bellicosity of most of his advisers.

In an early press conference that fall, Kennedy had boxed himself in by vowing to prohibit the introduction of "offensive weapons" into Cuba. Shipping intelligence, agent reports, and CIA's U-2 flights over the island were all employed to detect and verify the presence of such weapons.

But there were some special problems.

McNamara versus McCone

In the Kennedy administration, the entrenched institutional rivalry of the Pentagon and CIA was fortified by a personal contest between McNamara and McCone over their respective peacetime and wartime roles. An accomplished bureaucratic aggrandizer, McCone satisfied himself that, in wartime, many of McNamara's peacetime responsibilities for the budgets and personnel of major electronic and technical intelligence collection would legally shift to McCone. McNamara naturally resisted this rather transparent trespass.

To the amusement of his colleagues, McCone also had occasional trouble with his syntax. "We've got to watch out for Indians like Christian (Krishna) Menon who are not revelant (sic) to nucular (sic) weapons..."

In September, 1962, McCone announced that, contrary to official CIA views, his personal opinion was that the Soviets intended to send offensive missiles into Cuba. Undeterred by the implications of his own estimate that we were therefore on the threshold of nuclear war, McCone then took off for a month's honeymoon on the Riviera. McNamara, by then no friend of the CIA director, told Rusk that he suspected McCone was a double-entry bookkeeper, who wrote two memos with opposite predictions, put them in his desk drawer, and when one of them turned out to be accurate, shredded the other.

★ ★ ★

Scheduling With Mixed Motives

On September 10, 1962, a fateful meeting was requested by McGeorge Bundy and Dean Rusk. They contacted Jim Reber at CIA, the head of COMOR (the Committee on Overhead Reconnaissance). He was technically responsible for proposing U-2 flights over Cuba, and was instructed to come to the Bundy office to discuss U-2 scheduling.

Bundy and Rusk were both worried. In 1961 the CIA and the Air Force had been accused of "entrapment" of the President at the Bay of Pigs, deliberately putting him in the position of either using force to salvage a desperate situation or backing down. Bundy and Rusk had been criticized severely for their passivity in failing to protect Kennedy at that time. The two men also remembered that there had been a serious international uproar after the Soviet shoot-down of Gary Powers and his U-2 in 1960. There had been no subsequent flights over the USSR.

But in August, 1962, another American U-2 had strayed over Soviet Sakhalin. A Chinese Nationalist U-2 had been shot down over the China mainland on September 9, the day before the requested meeting. Rusk feared that the clamor over a new U-2 incident would not only jeopardize further U-2 flights over Cuba, but might jeopardize his Berlin negotiations and a prospective nuclear test ban treaty with the Soviets.

Bundy and Rusk knew that hawks in the US government had regularly pressed for more U-2 fights over Cuba, hoping for a shoot-down that would provoke a US invasion. In September, both men also accepted the common wisdom that it was unlikely that the Soviets would place offensive missiles in Cuba. Another special national intelligence estimate would reinforce that view on September 19, nine days later.

In asking for the meeting, Bundy and Rusk also inquired of Reber whether there was anyone involved in the planning of the U-2 missions who might want to provoke an incident, a US air strike, or a US invasion of Cuba. As it turned out, the embodiment of that suspicion appeared in person as a fourth participant in the meeting.

Reber's superior, General "Pat" Carter, fitted the provocateur prescription perfectly. "Let's arrange an incident at Guantanamo. Let's fly even lower level planes to increase the chance of a shoot-down. What do we need? A Republican Congress in order to declare war?" His hawkish views were certainly known to Reber. Carter's attendance at the meeting, however, was of an accidental, surrogate nature. He was acting DCI, because CIA Director McCone was away on his honeymoon.

A fifth participant in the meeting was also known for his bellicosity, Attorney General Robert Kennedy. Thus it happened that the Big 4 at Reber's September 10th meeting— Bundy, Rusk, Carter, and Kennedy– held conflicting views and motivations going well beyond Reber's technical assignment of U-2 scheduling.

A spirited discussion featured Rusk's and Bundy's anxieties over the international and domestic risks of unbridled U-2 flights over Cuba. Bobby typically complained: "What no guts, Dean?" His objections subsided when Rusk and Bundy explained that they were trying to save his brother from entrapment. Finally Carter and Kennedy reluctantly accepted two peripheral flights and two in-and-out missions as substitutes for full-scale U2 flights over the island.

This did attenuate the U-2 schedule. It arguably postponed the definitive discovery of offensive missiles until October 14th. But when Reber saw Carter, his chief, acceding to the new arrangements, he got the message and accommodated them in his own timetable. It was a fateful and fortuitous combination of people whose personal agendas only partially connected with the technical agenda for U-2 scheduling.

★ ★ ★

Hazardous Briefings

In the middle of the second week of the missile crisis, the President decided that the nation's governors, senators, and congressmen should be cultivated. White House telegrams went out asking them all to break off their election campaigns and come either to New York or Chicago on Thursday, October 25th, to be briefed about the missile crisis. The day before, Kennedy called TLH and asked him to do the briefings.

Reading the NY Times in the plane to New York on Thursday morning, TLH discovered that almost all of his prepared briefing was in the newspaper. Scores of politicians en route would be reading the Times as well. TLH needed something more. Reached by phone, Roger Hilsman, then INR director, suggested that TLH could mention that a Soviet tanker, the Bucharest, was approaching the quarantine line en route to Havana, and that the Excom in the White House was currently grappling with a proper response.

TLH's high level audience began taking their places at the federal court house in New York City. Nelson Rockefeller, Abe Ribicoff, Prescott Bush, John Rooney and Peter Rodino were conspicuous in the front row. All had signed a classified document recognizing that the briefing was top secret. After mentioning the Bucharest, TLH failed to notice the quiet departure of Congressman van Zandt, who was running for the Senate in Pennsylvania. Addressing a bevy of television cameras outside the briefing room, he announced that the Bucharest, a Soviet ship, was nearing the quarantine line and that the dithering Kennedy administration couldn't make up its mind whether to board it, blow it up, or let it pass. Van Zandt's TV appearance was beamed directly into the White House meeting and the President went through the roof.

Unaware of all this, TLH finished his briefing and headed back to LaGuardia. The airport was in turmoil. American Airlines personnel in their brown uniforms were prancing around announcing solemnly: "It's the President for American passenger Hughes. It's President Kennedy calling American Airlines. It's American. Will American passenger Hughes report at once to the American counter? It's the President. It's American." Personnel from the other airlines looked dejected.

TLH rushed to the American counter. "President Kennedy wants you to call him immediately. There's a booth right over there." After putting a dime in the pay phone, TLH reached the New York operator. "I want to call President Kennedy immediately, collect." "You WHAT?" she exclaimed. "The President wants me to call him at once." "He does, does he?" "Look, Miss, it's urgent. If you can't get through to the President himself, I'll talk to his secretary, Mrs. Lincoln." "Mrs. LINCOLN!"

Finally Kennedy came on the line, much agitated. "What the hell is going on up there? I don't know whose fool idea it was to brief all those politicians! Everyone knows they can't keep a secret!" TLH: "In a calmer moment, Mr. President, I'll be glad to review the bidding. The immediate question is: do you want me to go on to Chicago where 250 more of them are waiting, or should we cancel?" (Pause). "Oh what the hell, Tom, better go ahead. Just don't let any more of them get on TV!

You understand?" "Of course, Mr. President. Right, Mr. President."

The Scali Gambit

TLH returned to Washington late Thursday night and spent Friday working with John Scali of ABC who had been contacted by the KGB chief at the Soviet Embassy, Alexander Fomin. He had claimed to have a direct line to the Kremlin and was testing a proposal for resolving the crisis. TLH and Scali went together to see Rusk who prepared a positive message in return. He wanted to exploit all possible avenues to Khrushchev.

The trip away from Washington had forced TLH to give up tickets for "Iolanthe," the Gilbert & Sullivan production at the National Theater. In compensation the Hughes family were given tickets for "The Mikado" matinee on Saturday afternoon, October 27. This was the worst day of the missile crisis. At the end of act one, the Lord High Executioner came out on the stage and announced: "If there is a Thomas Hughes in the audience, he is to go at once to the White House." It was another Scali report, and the two men went in together to brief Dean Rusk on the KGB's latest message from Moscow.

The Missile Crisis Aftermath

After the crisis subsided, the State Department in its wisdom gave TLH an award bearing the rather ambiguous inscription:

"To Thomas L. Hughes for his contribution to the Cuba missile crisis."

In 1964, after he had left the government, Roger Hilsman wrote an article on the missile crisis for Look Magazine. The account disclosed the Scali episodes, and Dean Rusk was deeply upset. He turned to two State Department lawyers— Daniel Davidson and Abe Chayes—for legal advice on whether Hilsman had committed a criminal offense. Both lawyers promptly said no, he could not be prosecuted under the Espionage Act as Rusk had hoped.

Sober Afterthoughts

Two weeks later, after the Cuba Missile Crisis subsided, TLH was on Air Force reserve duty in Puerto Rico. The then Governor Luis Munoz Marin, a good friend of Chester Bowles, invited TLH for a private visit to his country place at Trujillo Alto on a Sunday afternoon. The founding father of the Commonwealth of Puerto Rico began by saying, with reference to Kennedy, Khrushchev, and the missile crisis: "Tom, it is a sobering afterthought, is it not, that the survival of humanity these days depends upon the Irish and the Slavs!"

At that point TLH did not yet know that Khrushchev was already writing personally to Kennedy post-crisis, warning him to stop needling Castro at his press conferences. "Castro and his young friends are excitable, impulsive, and sudden—in short, Spaniards!" Had he known, Munoz probably would have been happy to include his own ethnic cohorts in his sobering thought.

For TLH this was the beginning of many decades of involvement in Puerto Rico, including the restoration of two Spanish colonial houses in Old San Juan. Governor Rafael Hernandez-Colon later appointed TLH co-chairman of his Committee on US-Puerto Rico Relations, which sponsored cultural events at the Metropolitan in New York and at galleries in San Juan.

Official Views in Panama

TLH's 9999th AF Reserve Squadron went on to visit Panama that December of 1962. The visit started with Ambassador Farland who sat at his desk beneath a picture of J Edgar Hoover. Farland said that for fifty years the local school children had been drilled to demand renegotiation of the canal treaty. "They are all little treaty experts. In fact 60-70% of the high school student body is communist. Curacao is the exit point for them going to Cuba, Moscow, and Peking for training."

In the Canal Zone, the commandant of the USAF School for Latin America was forthright enough. He talked about his Panama commando unit, saying (jokingly?) "They're passing their course in palace bombing. As soon as they complete their new loyalty checks, we'll be back in business. Insurgency is actually more fun than counter-insurgency.

"Counter-insurgency is basically a re-insurance policy for governments under fire. It reinforces the conservative elements in every country. So now we also have duties in Guatemala, Honduras, and the Dominican Republic. In fact, our special forces crews are training on the spot in ten Latin American countries this year.

"Sometimes we must embolden reactionary governments in decline by creating feelings of dependency and reliance on the US. For example, we can supply photos of President Kennedy to hang on the wall with Somoza in Nicaragua and Stroessner in Paraguay. As Kennedy said to the Latin American heads of state on his visit: 'You and I leave here today to meet our separate responsibilities–to protect our vital interests by resolute action if necessary. Success to you all in your respective fatherlands'."

The commandant concluded: "And another thing. Why are we supposed to worry about testing nuclear weapons? General LeMay himself went out to the test range and found that only the land crabs were a little hot."

A Canal Zone Cocktail Hour

The cocktail party featured General Stranathan, Congressman Whitener of North Carolina, Congressman Clark of Pennsylvania, Mrs. Colonel W, and Mrs. Colonel R. "Handling" the crisis in Panama was the subject of the day.

As the "Negro waiter" passed the French pastries, Congressman Whitener said: "The only thing these people understand is skull-cracking…Let me have one of the goodiest of the goodies. I'll take two. I can't figure which is the goodiest."

When the commanding general arrived, Whitener exclaimed: "General, I wouldn't ordinarily mention it, but one of these beautiful ladies just said: "Oh, Mr. Congressman, I just adore working on this base under General Stranathan. Now didn't one of you beautiful ladies just say that? Oh! Oh! Now, you know I'd never tell which."

Mrs. Colonel R: "It just doesn't feel right to have the addressees in the states pay duty on a US product bought in our Panama PX and shipped back home. Congressman, can't you do something about that? There are socialists everywhere. The University of Panama, of course, is heavily communist infiltrated."

Congressman Clark: "How did we ever let that happen? As long as a friendly Latin American military revolts and sets itself up, that's o.k. with me. As long as they remain friendly, that is. There's nothing wrong with a friendly revolution."

General Stranathan: "The key to our approach is indoctrinating the future leaders. There were riots in six Latin American countries when the Bay of Pigs occurred. We want to be sure we're protected against that next time. We are militarily prepared to intervene wherever and whenever the President tells us to. As for me, I'm retiring in the spring to Abilene, taking a few folksy symbolic things back with me, of course."

Mrs. Colonel W: "Don't you think, Randy, this stone is too large?" Randy: "No ring is too large." Mrs. Colonel W: "Of course, it's not a precious stone. And her green one over there is lighter than my blue. But my husband is just the best shopper when he goes to Lima. When the jeweler here saw this, he said: 'Insure it for $500. That's what I'd sell it for.' Randy paid $15. The jeweler said: 'Buy me all you can on your next TDY'."

Mrs. Colonel R, after getting a second helping for Congressman Whitener: "It's our zone, our property. It just sticks in my craw that those communists in our State Department made us put up the Panama flag." Both Congressmen, in unison: "How many places are both flags flying?"

Mrs. Colonel R: "Thank God, only two. Governor Fleming took down his flag pole. Better fly nothing than both. I certainly am going to miss fishing off the Governor's boat."

Congressman Whitener: "How I wish I had bought some of that German communist Meissen china that Bill Scranton bought last year. Of course, Mrs. Whitener wanted more of the silver service too. But I said why? Isn't three dozen place settings enough?"

Mrs. Colonel W: (seeking out Colonel Walter Jenkins, LBJ's assistant): "Please tell that boss of yours that we love that Lyndon! Tell him that last month everyone here from Texas was looking forward to the thrill of some action for our boys in Cuba. My, were we disappointed! I'm sure that ol' Lyndon wouldn't have allowed that to happen."

Mrs. Colonel R: "Everybody here knows that there have been missiles in Cuba since 1960. My husband and I have two sons in the army, and we knew that their futures were at stake— their promotions, that is. We were hoping for their baptism of fire. When we saw the ships going through the Canal we all said Go, Go, Go. We were all War Hawks. How shameful it all was."

Mrs. Colonel W: "I hope you all will go back and tell people that down here we don't want our military budgets diverted into soft goods. We don't believe in racial mixing, half-breeds, civic action and all these new concepts. Does Mr. Moscoso from Puerto Rico really understand that? Actually some campesinos here did begin to pass information to our military attaches. The problem is that they then got shot."

Dallas

TLH returned from Europe on November 21, 1963. As his plane was landing at Andrews Air Force Base, Air Force One was on the adjoining runway, taking off for Texas, bearing President Kennedy to his fateful rendezvous. Adlai Stevenson and others had specifically warned about the dangers in Dallas, but the imperatives of Texas politics had overridden all the warning signs in favor of the President's trip.

A Funereal Gathering

In the grief-stricken days after the Kennedy assassination, the State Department was responsible for handing the influx of foreign dignitaries who came to pay their respects. After the funeral at St. Matthew's Cathedral, the official guests all repaired to the State Department's diplomatic reception rooms, where assistant secretaries of state were instructed to look after their needs and make them feel as comfortable as possible with one another.

One of the guests, General De Gaulle, required delicate handling. The Elysee Treaty between France and West Germany had been signed earlier that year. After succeeding Adenauer as chancellor, Ludwig Erhard had publicly supported the US on Vietnam. He was promptly informed by De Gaulle that this transgression violated the Elysee Treaty. The adverse reaction to De Gaulle in Washington was predictable.

After the Kennedy funeral, TLH was assigned not only to De Gaulle, but to another imperial potentate, Emperor Haile Selassie. The 6' x 6" French head of state towered above the 5' x 4" miniature Ethiopian. Fortunately the emperor spoke a kind of French, so the general could accept a proper obeisance from him in the universal language. But theirs was a rather stiff discourse at the reception, until Prince Philip wandered over to join them, prompting a language switch to English.

Admiring and Accepting Gift Horses

"You see a lot of horses," the Aga Khan used to remark, "and some say something to you, and some don't." Admiring other people's horses was a rewarding habit for several prominent Americans in the post-war world. The polo-playing Averell Harriman, for example, knew a good horse when he saw one. When he was ambassador in Moscow, he told Stalin how much he admired a certain Red Army stallion that he had seen on parade. Stalin took the hint and gave the horse to Averell, along with another for his daughter Kathleen. Apparently unworried about accusations of impropriety, the Harrimans had no qualms about accepting gift horses from the Russians. "Reverse Lend Lease" they called it.

During his state visit to Washington in July 1961, the Pakistani president, Ayub Khan, was the guest of honor at a lavish formal dinner laid on at Mount Vernon, the only such state dinner there in history. On her own visit to Pakistan in March, 1962, Jackie accepted a gift horse from Ayub. When President Kennedy raised his eyebrows about the propriety of his wife's accepting the gift, Jackie settled the matter: "But I WANT the horse!"

Lyndon Johnson was also a horse admirer, but a less successful one. Once when he was in Puerto Rico, he reviewed a parade in the Plaza de Armas in Old San Juan. A prancing Palomino suddenly caught his eye. "Ah'd like that one" LBJ explained to the mayor. The owner of the horse was told that he could contribute to the betterment of North American-Puerto Rican relations by surrendering his horse to Johnson, but he declined the honor. The high level visitor from Washington was not amused.

Fortunately for all concerned, LBJ's great friend Abe Fortas was also the lawyer for Puerto Rico. He intervened on the island's behalf and prevented retribution.

Johnson was more successful later on when it came to appropriating helicopters. When advised by his military aide at a busy base that "your helicopter is over there, Mr. President," the commander-in-chief famously responded: "Son, they're all my helicopters."

III

JOHNSON'S WHITE HOUSE YEARS
1963-69
★ ★ ★

"Keep Him Fo' Me"

Johnson's possessiveness was not limited to horses and helicopters. After the Kennedy assassination, TLH and his wife went to the White House reception for sub-Cabinet officials, the first one held in the Johnson presidency. After a brief exchange with Lady Bird in the receiving line, they were face-to-face with the new president. Gripping Jean's small extended hand between his two enormous ones, he said to her in his Texas drawl: "Keep him fo' me." As they moved on, Jean exclaimed rather distinctly: "What the hell did he say?" LBJ overheard her from several feet away and interrupted his hand-shaking. He came down the line to confront the Hugheses again: "AH SAY'ed, KEEP HIM FO' ME."

As the Vietnam crisis deepened, it became abundantly clear what being kept for LBJ really meant. There exists a memo from Bill Moyers to McGeorge Bundy that literally reads: "The President asked me to tell you that he wants— 'by the time I get up in the morning'—everything every

Republican Senator and Congressman—and Democrats alike—said, which indicates that SEATO requires us to give arms to SEATO countries—the whole debate—everything Eisenhower said in office that builds our case—the full text of his letter to Churchill and Diem. I want the kind of brief Abe Fortas would prepare. It's got to be full and convincing. Then I want General Goodpasture (Goodpaster–LBJ always enjoyed deliberately distorting personal names) to helicopter up to Gettysburg tomorrow. I want him to take all the material that Mac Bundy is going to get overnight. Tell Mac to get that fellow Tom Hughes out of bed over at State and make him do all this research tonight, him and his people."

★ ★ ★

Mann versus Marx

As the dictator Porfirio Diaz used to say, "Poor Mexico: so far from God, so close to the United States." In the early 1960s, that thought occurred to visitors to the American Embassy in Mexico City. Outside the office of Ambassador Tom Mann were autobiographical pamphlets disclosing his view of his own role in Mexico: "Mann versus Marx."

Among the very first moves of his presidency, Lyndon Johnson appointed Mann, a fellow Texan, to be his personal representative at the State Department. To start with, Mann was given three simultaneous appointments: Assistant Secretary for Inter-American Affairs, Special Assistant to the President, and head of the Alliance for Progress (AID administrator). Later he became Undersecretary of State. These wide-ranging assignments were understood to include clearing out leftist suspects whose views might not coincide with new

Johnsonian White House policies—including, especially, clearing out any prominent, but suspect, Kennedy appointees,

The Importance of Household Effects

It happened that in early December, 1963, Dean Rusk had prematurely taken Ambassador Murat Williams (an FSO) over to the White House to introduce him to LBJ as our new ambassador to the Dominican Republic. A few days later, Williams unfortunately came to Tom Mann's attention. He identified Murat with Kennedy and the Alliance for Progress. Murat had been JFK's ambassador to Salvador, where his liberal record had offended the "Fourteen Families," who were accustomed to running the country.

Mann suddenly interrupted a morning briefing by TLH to say that he had to dictate a memo. TLH started to leave, but was asked to remain. The memo would just take a minute, but it disclosed how the new broom would sweep. Mann proceeded to dictate for the files: "I have had occasion to compare the cost of shipping the household effects of the Murat Williamses from Salvador to the Dominican Republic with the cost of shipping the household effects of the Tapley Bennetts from Athens to the Dominican Republic. I find that it is cheaper to ship them from Athens. Therefore Tapley Bennett will be our new ambassador to the Dominican Republic."

Political protection became important in such situations in 1964, and certain precautions were taken. For instance, when TLH considered asking Murat Williams to join INR as a deputy director that year, the two men first paid a visit to Attorney General Kennedy to acquaint him with all the background that preceded Murat's joining INR– in effect obtaining a second blessing of the new arrangement.

What and Whom to Ignore

Tom Mann's assignment extended far beyond Latin America. Bob Good, for example, was one of the nation's most respected academic experts on Africa. TLH had been instrumental in appointing him office director for African Affairs in INR where he had served brilliantly for several years. Although a non-FSO, he had subsequently been appointed ambassador to Zambia. Tom Mann had never met him, but Mann's verdict on him was clear enough: "Of course, we don't have a professional out there, so we can discount Embassy Lusaka's reporting." Mann's map of the world sharply divided not only anti-Communists from pro-Communists, and suspected Kennedites from known Johnsonites, but also FSOs from all "non-professionals."

Exit Abba Schwartz

Another early victim, ferreted out by Tom Mann's sleuthing in 1964, was the Kennedy's administration's Assistant Secretary for Security, Abba Schwartz. In addition to his friendship with Attorney General Kennedy, one of Abba's other shortcomings was his meddling in the domain of Frances Knight, who was still on the State Department payroll and who enjoyed a new lease on life when LBJ succeeded JFK. After being fired, Abba was presented with a gilded 8" x 10" heraldic wall decoration at his departure ceremony. It bore the inscription: "Once a King always a King, but once a Knight is enough."

A Swimming Pool Saga

Once in a while, unclassified information of a sensational nature also came into his hands and TLH was able to pass it on to the press. One such occasion is recounted by Max Frankel of the New York Times in his autobiography.

"My all-time favorite piece of 'deep background' news was acquired at the very deep end of our Chevy Chase neighborhood swimming pool on a very hot Sunday afternoon in June, 1964. The Frankels were there and so were Madie and Marvin Kalb of CBS and other reporters and quite a few government officials.

"Treading water after a lap or two, I encountered Tom Hughes, the head of intelligence and research at the State Department and a close associate of soon-to-be Vice President Hubert Humphrey. Hughes could hardly contain his amusement at a cable the night before from Henry Cabot Lodge, the liberal Republican then serving as Lyndon Johnson's ambassador to South Vietnam. Obviously eager to get home to contest the nomination of Barry Goldwater, Lodge was asking to be relieved within thirty days and allowed to plead not politics but reasons of health.

"Wow! Can I use that?" "Just leave me out of it," Hughes replied. Not knowing whether we'd been observed in the pool, I rejoined our family circle in the grass and played conspicuously with all the little Frankels. Not until an hour

later did I amble to a phone, dictate a lengthy story direct
to New York, and amble back into the pool. The story—
LODGE RESIGNING; EXPECTED HOME FOR
CONVENTION—led the Times the next morning."

★ ★ ★

LBJ Learns about the Gulf of Tonkin

Around 6 a.m. on August 2, 1964, TLH was awakened by his
White House phone. It was the opening day of the Gulf of
Tonkin crisis. Unfortunately many of the President's closest
advisers were away. McNamara was climbing mountains in
Wyoming. The Bundy brothers and McCone were also out
of town. When TLH reported to Dean Rusk's house for
breakfast, he found a motley group already there with Rusk—
McNamara's deputy Cyrus Vance, Rusk's deputy George Ball,
General Wheeler (the new Chairman of the Joint Chiefs of
Staff), and two technicians from the Navy and CIA. It was
daybreak in Washington when the first reports of an attack
had come in.

While Virginia Rusk cooked breakfast, the group studied
maps of the Gulf of Tonkin, tried to estimate how many miles
from shore the USS Maddox had been, and speculated about
the effect of islands on claims of territorial waters. Armed
with tentative information, the participants dispersed to their
respective offices for the latest intelligence. Then, around 11
a.m., they reconvened at the White House to brief President
Johnson.

It was a session full of levity. Johnson looked over his
motley group of visitors, and began by asking: "Where're my
Bundys?" Answering his own question, he continued: "Ah

know. They're up there at that female island of their's (Martha's Vineyard). That's where they are, playing tennis this very minute, up there at that female island."

"Now, what's the big emergency?" The sailor popped up, saluted, and said: "Well, Mr. President, one of our destroyers has been attacked." Johnson: "One of our destroyers? Attacked? Now who would do a damn fool thing like that?" The sailor continued: "It's the North Vietnamese, Mr. President. We have shells from their torpedo boats." "What more do we know?" "That is all we know at the moment, Mr. President, but as soon as we have something more, we'll bring it to your attention right away." The sailor saluted again and sat down.

After a pause, Johnson inquired: "We weren't up to any mischief out there, were we?" Another pause. Then Ball said: "Well, you remember, Mr. President, that you signed off on those 34-A operations last December, that were recommendations left over from the previous administration." "Ah did? Now remind me what those 34-A operations do." Vance explained that the American hand didn't show. They were totally disavowable. They were run strictly by the South Vietnamese. "Sometimes they blow up a bridge, capture a fisherman, or maybe light up the radar along the coasts."

"Light up the radar?" said the President. "So if we just happened to have a destroyer in the area, we could maybe map the coast electronically?" "Maybe," the group agreed. "Now could any of those 34-A operations have occurred recently?" The sailor jumped up again, saluted, and said: "Well, Sir, of course we don't keep track of all those missions in Washington. That's CINCPAC's responsibility, yes, CINCPAC out in Hawaii. But it could be that they had an operation a couple of nights ago." "Ah see," said Johnson, "a couple of nights ago. And that's all we know?" "Yes, Sir, that's all we know."

Like the Movies in Texas

"Well," said the President, "it reminds me of goin' to the movies in Texas. You're sittin' there next to a pretty girl and you have your hand on her ankle. And nothin' happens. You move your hand up to her calf. And nothin' happens. You move your hand up to her knee, and still nothin' happens. And you're thinking about movin' it higher, when, all of a sudden, you get slapped. Ah' think we just got slapped."

Then LBJ briefly left the room, leaving the group admiring his succinct and professional diagnosis of the situation. TLH penciled a note for the Secretary of State, and pushed it across the table to Rusk: "Now that we know what happens at the movies in Texas, do you wish to continue to call this an unprovoked attack?" Not particularly amused, Rusk said: "We'll ask Cy Vance. He's our lawyer." Turning to Vance, Rusk said: "This was an unprovoked attack, wouldn't you agree, Cy?" Rising to the occasion with a superb non sequitur, Vance replied: "Of course it was unprovoked. It occurred in international waters."

Turning to Something Serious

Having returned to the room, President Johnson observed: "It seems a bit murky. So we won't have any retaliation, but we will warn them against doing anything further. Now let's turn to something serious." He meant the postal pay bill. Turning to his newly appointed chairman of the Joint Chiefs of Staff, he said: "Now, General Wheeler, you're my new chief strategic adviser. This postal pay bill is marchin' down Pennsylvania Avenue toward the White House. It's already at 9th street, movin' on 10th. Your President—and, General, you have only one President—is damned if he signs it, and damned if he vetoes it. General, your President needs your best strategic advice."

General Wheeler had never before been called on to advise on postal pay matters, and he fumbled around miserably. Johnson became impatient. "General, Ah sure hope Ah haven't made a mistake. You've been wasting my time. That bill is already at 12th Street, movin' toward 13th." The meeting ended in an inconclusive uproar. At the door as he was leaving, a red-faced General Wheeler asked plaintively of nobody in particular: "Is it always like this?"

That was Act 1 of the Gulf of Tonkin saga. Johnson sized up the situation accurately, acted with restraint, and avoided escalation. Ironically he responded to a phantom attack two days later. He thought it was genuine, and sent his fateful Tonkin Gulf resolution up to Capitol Hill.

★ ★ ★

Briefing HHH at Atlantic City

Later that same month, after much orchestrated suspense, LBJ chose Humphrey to be his running mate for the fall elections. As Director of INR, TLH was asked to brief his old friend Humphrey during the campaign. His briefings on foreign intelligence were scheduled to start at the Democratic national convention in Atlantic City the day of the Vice Presidential nomination. At that particular moment, however, Hubert was naturally less interested in foreign intelligence than in preparing his acceptance speech. He asked his entourage for suggestions. TLH remembered Emerson's phrase about the two contesting parties that divided mankind—"the Party of Hope and the Party of Memory." Humphrey liked that theme, used it in his acceptance speech, and reaped editorial praise in the major papers the following morning.

At the same time the administration offered TLH as the foreign intelligence briefing officer to Goldwater, now the Republican presidential nominee. He had been the commanding general of TLH's Air Force Reserve unit, which had just been disbanded by McNamara. But Goldwater politely declined, preferring, everyone assumed, to get his intelligence directly from his buddy, General Curtis LeMay. Despite this, the LBJ-HHH ticket went on to a big victory in November.

Neutralizing the Walter Jenkins Alarm

When the Walter Jenkins scandal broke, involving a sexual encounter in the men's room at the YMCA, LBJ was beside himself. It was already mid-October, at the height of the 1964 election season. The media coverage of the debacle of LBJ's faithful aide threatened to halt the momentum of Johnson's otherwise triumphant campaign.

TLH happened to be at the White House for a meeting with Harry McPherson when the Jenkins crisis was at its height. Johnson was expecting a Jenkins-oriented attack from Goldwater at any minute. TLH knew what the White House apparently did not know: that Jenkins had been a member of Goldwater's 9999th Air Force Reserve squadron, and that in all likelihood Goldwater, as his commanding officer, had signed off for years on Jenkins' personal effectiveness reports.

McPherson sent a note in to the President with this information, and suddenly there was a whoop and a holler from inside the Oval Office. The Pentagon was urgently asked to document this gift from the gods, and the White House was soon in a position to inform the Goldwater campaign that there probably would not be much mileage to be gained in their attempting to exploit the Jenkins matter.

Another Fateful Memo.

After the election, with his friend Humphrey now assuming the Vice Presidency, TLH was immediately typed as Humphrey's man at the State Department. TLH also found himself in the center of policy controversies that divided the Vice President's own staff. The most immediate one was LBJ's threatened escalation in Vietnam. Hawkish advisers were in the majority in the White House and also in Humphrey's own office.

At a National Security Council meeting on February 10, when asked their opinion by LBJ, Humphrey and George Ball had been alone in opposing proposed air strikes on North Vietnam while Soviet Premier Kosygin was visiting Hanoi. Three days later on February 13, Humphrey was not invited to an important follow-up meeting at the White House. That night TLH phoned the Vice President stressing the urgency of his reading recent Vietnam-related cables, INR memos, and new national intelligence estimates which raised grave doubts about the probable consequences of escalation. Humphrey was heading for a quiet weekend in Georgia and asked TLH to join him there.

The two men were alone for a day and a half, and at the end they composed an extensive and prophetic 12-point memo from Humphrey to Johnson. It is reprinted in Humphrey's memoirs ("The Education of a Public Man" p. 320-4.). Totally prescient about what would happen on the American domestic scene if the Vietnam War were to escalate, the memo precisely predicts the domestic political reaction which in fact did occur, and which probably kept Humphrey from winning his own race for the White House in 1968.

In February, 1965, Johnson's reaction was explosive. He didn't appreciate cautious advice, even from his number 2, and, in effect, he banned Humphrey from major foreign policy meetings for the following year. Humphrey paid the price of resuming tolerable relations with LBJ by supporting the Vietnam War, just as it went from bad to worse.

LBJ Finds a New CIA Director

In early 1965 LBJ also had to find a successor for John McCone as CIA director. Johnson turned to John Macy, his headhunter, saying: "Find me an admiral who voted for us last November." "An ADMIRAL who voted for YOU, Mr. President?" "You heard what Ah say-ed."

In due course, newsmen and intelligence chiefs were summoned to the White House for the unveiling of Admiral "Red" Raborn from Texas as the new CIA director. It was explained that he was the inventor of the Polaris submarine. "Ah've bin searchin' high and low, east and west, all over this great land, to get just the right man for the CIA. When duty called, he accepted. Here he is now…" The press was correctly skeptical of much of this story, but attributed it to LBJ's well-known hyperbole.

Raborn Gets Right to Work.

A week later, the Admiral told TLH what happened next. "I went right back to the Agency and went into my Operations Center. Suddenly I read on the tickers that the communists were taking over the Dominican Republic. I thought to myself, there's no time to lose. I ripped the message off the ticker and phoned the President right away. I told him that as his new DCI, I was action-oriented. We can't have another Cuba in the Caribbean. The Commies were on the move, and our men would have to go. He said he would call me back in fifteen minutes. He did. "They're on their way," he said.

"So the Dominican invasion was decided without the participation of the State Department, the Pentagon, the CIA, or the White House staff? Just you, Red, and the President?" "That's right, Tom. I'm action-oriented."

It had been a perfectly fact-free invasion.

A Versatile DCI

A month or so later, TLH was in Williamsburg to speak
at a large gathering of the military-industrial complex. At
the conference dinner he was seated next to Wernher von
Braun, Hitler's former rocket chief, now master-minding
our space program. Von Braun had started to explain
how the Bible had always guided him in his important
decisions. Suddenly this potentially fascinating disclosure of
theological inspiration at Peenemuende was interrupted by
events on the stage.

Out came a harpist with her harp, followed by a figure who
looked familiar. "Is that who I think it is?" von Braun asked.
"Yes, I am afraid it is our new Director of Central Intelligence,
Admiral Raborn." "But is he going to sing for us?" "I'm afraid
so." The admiral's vigorous renditions of "Danny Boy" and
"When Irish Eyes are Smiling" evoked a wistful reaction from
the German missile man who sighed: "As Goethe once put it,
'America, you have it better'."

A Mission to San Juan

As the weeks went by, Johnson apparently came to think
that more than Raborn's help was needed, and he decided to
send three of his trusted advisors down to San Juan to talk to
the exiled Dominican president, Juan Bosch, and find some
way to end the American military intrusion. The three were
McGeorge Bundy from the White House, George Ball from
State, and Justice Abe Fortas (now a Supreme Court justice,
but a regular Presidential confidant after hours.)

In the last days of the Kennedy administration, sources in the White House had spread the word that Dean Rusk would not be kept on in a second Kennedy term. In response Rusk had let it be known that he was really too poor financially to remain. Bundy, Ball and Fortas would each happily have been Rusk's successor. For Bundy and Ball, this contingency was one of the factors that made staying around in the Johnson administration worthwhile.

Going on a diplomatic errand to Bosch also happened to fit the efforts of each of the envoys to break out of his respective Vietnam stereotype and display new wisdom and breadth of character. Thus Bundy, a hawk on Vietnam, became a dove on the Dominican Republic. Fortas, the biggest hawk in town on Vietnam, also became a dove on the DR. Ball, the dove on Vietnam, became a hawk on the DR. Each was eager to broaden his reputation as a qualifier for higher office.

It occurred to the President that J Edgar Hoover might also play a positive role in all this. Before long an intelligence board meeting was briefed on the particulars by William Sullivan, the FBI deputy director who himself hoped to succeed Hoover. LBJ invited Hoover to tape the conversations of his three emissaries in Puerto Rico. Hoover was thrilled because he had always yearned to resume a more active role in the hemisphere. It had been an area of proprietary FBI interest, before the CIA had edged them out.

★ ★ ★

Where's My Bundy?

Up in the White House family quarters the first night, LBJ and the FBI director rejoiced over the initial batch of tapes.

They chortled over how dovish Fortas had become, and how hawkish Ball had become. But on the second night, LBJ asked: "Where's my Bundy? Know he's down there. Sent him down there." Chastised, Hoover rushed back to the fortress to find out what had happened to the Bundy tapes. After turning the place upside down, the FBI belatedly discovered that Bundy was speaking Spanish, a language then apparently unknown at FBI headquarters.

Even worse, Bundy's caper violated the Director's insistence on a "level playing field" between the tapers and the taped. Spanish translators had to be brought in, on an emergency basis, to find out what LBJ's national security adviser was up to.

Hoover volunteered that he had never trusted McGeorge Bundy anyway, "ever since that crack of his about his religion." "Oh, what was that?" inquired LBJ. "Well, Bundy was asked how fervent an Episcopalian he actually was. The smart aleck replied: 'Confirmed, but not convinced.' Not very funny, if you ask me," said the FBI director.

Rivals for an Un-Vacant Chair

These three Presidential advisers had also underestimated the staying power of Dean Rusk. LBJ's ascendancy had been, in fact, a lucky break for Rusk. The Secretary was suddenly comfortable with his boss. He and Johnson came from similar rural southern backgrounds. Both had Confederate forbears. LBJ said "Ah always feel more comfortable when Dean Rusk comes into the room." Rusk himself stopped referring to his departure, and was showing more interest in his own longevity as Secretary of State. In his desk he kept a list of his predecessors. He once proudly told TLH "Tom, I've just passed Frelinghuysen."

The Mixed Manned Boat

McGeorge Bundy and George Ball never disguised their rivalry. Shortly after Johnson's inauguration in late January, 1965, TLH was summoned to the White House to Mac Bundy's basement office to discuss the MLF—the Multilateral Force, the State Department's ill fated proposal for multi-national, mix-manned vessels carrying nuclear weapons. It was a pet project of George Ball's, ostensibly designed to prevent further nuclear proliferation. With a smile, Bundy confided: "George just insists on being the piano payer on the MLF, doesn't he? Between you and me, we're about to scuttle that boat." The whole MLF proposition fell part a week later, right on time.

Bundy Recommends His Successor

About this same time, on February 2, 1965, Mac Bundy wrote Johnson recommending TLH—or, alternatively, Bill Moyers or Abram Chayes– "to come in as deputy in this office with a prospect of succession" when he, Bundy, should leave the White House. "I have mentioned Tom Hughes before. I continue to be deeply impressed by the range and fairness of his mind. He would have an instinctive understanding for the requirement that the man in this job must protect the President's right to hear both sides of the hard cases." Ironically, this was the same week that Bundy himself, after the attack at Pleiku in Vietnam, gave the President only one side of the case and pushed him strongly to begin bombing the North.

Lady Bird Hears the News

Joseph C. Harsch of the Christian Science Monitor told TLH that he had just been at the White House for lunch. He was sitting next to Lady Bird Johnson, when the butler came up to her bearing a message on a silver tray. The message said that she might want to know that Jackie Kennedy was announcing her engagement to Aristotle Onassis that afternoon. Lady Bird looked up at the butler and said, "Are you shittin' me?"

Mao Considers the Alternatives

That same week Chairman Mao reportedly granted a rare interview to a British diplomat in Peking, who asked: "What do you think would have happened if Chairman Khrushchev had been killed instead of President Kennedy?" Mao thought and replied: "I don't think that Mr. Onassis would have married Mrs. Khrushchev."

Rusk on Being Presidential

At staff meetings Rusk occasionally told his assistant secretaries: "Don't ask me what you should be worried about.

You tell me what I should be worried about. Naturally, give it prayerful Presbyterian consideration beforehand." One Saturday morning in June, 1965, TLH told Rusk, after prayerful consideration, that he should perhaps be aware that there was a growing inter-regional slump in staff morale in INR.

In February, 1965, LBJ had embarked on his dramatic escalation in Vietnam, and INR's Southeast Asian analysts found it hard to believe that he had read their warnings. In April, INR's South Asian analysts were startled by his abrupt cancellation of the Shastri and Ayub visits to Washington, because of their public opposition to US Vietnam policy. Then came his precipitous invasion of the Dominican Republic, and INR's Latin American analysts were similarly dismayed. So at least three regional offices in INR were restive over LBJ's recent initiatives.

"Oh, if people are unhappy," Rusk replied, "they should feel free to leave. We can always replace analysts." TLH said it wasn't quite so easy. There were real considerations of morale at issue. "Well, I hope they realize that there is a difference between intelligence and policy. A President has lots of things to consider besides intelligence in making up his mind."

Rusk then went on to contrast JFK and LBJ. "Let me tell you something. As you know, Tom, I am second to no one in my admiration for President Kennedy. (Really? TLH was thinking, maybe.) But President Kennedy was afraid to be president. He had won by such a narrow margin that he was immobilized. Now we have a man who is not afraid to be president. He has won by a big margin, and he is making big, presidential-sized, decisions. I hope analysts in INR realize that."

Vietnam's Social Toll

By 1966 Vietnam was breaking up social events in Washington. Gilbert Harrison had been a classmate of TLH at Oxford, and he was now the editor of the New Republic. He and his wife Nancy famously hosted an annual New Year's Eve party. Over the years it had included Republicans and Democrats, old and young, businessmen and labor leaders, typical of the inclusive social events that post-World War II Washington was accustomed to. Antagonisms over Vietnam, however, now took their toll. Bill Bundy, the Vietnam point man in State, and Mary Acheson, his wife, could not come if Eugene and Abigail McCarthy would be there, etc. Finally the Harrisons cancelled the whole event.

Vietnam's Inanimate Victims

Even furniture was not spared. One evening in 1967 there was a small dinner at the home of the correspondent of Paris Soir, Count Adalbert de Segonzac ("Ziggy") and his wife Madeleine. The guests included Walt Rostow, General Vernon Walters, TLH and their wives. After dinner the women were separated from the men as usual. In this case the men adjourned to Ziggy's study for brandy and cigars.

Vietnam quickly became the subject of animated argument. In the course of it, Rostow, emphasizing his steadfastness on Southeast Asia, brought his fist heavily down upon a fragile 18th century French side table. It splintered into tiny fragments.

The heavy General Walters joined Ziggy, Rostow, and Hughes on the floor, attempting to put Humpty-Dumpty together again. The Count de Segonzac lamented: "Walt, that poor table survived the French Revolution!" It was one more victim of Vietnam, thousands of miles away.

Soon afterwards Harris Wofford followed suit at a dinner at the Hughes home in Chevy Chase. Washington superlawyers Lloyd Cutler and Berl Bernhard, and their wives, were also present. Harris was castigating LBJ's bombing of North Vietnam. For emphasis, he lifted an antique Chippendale chair high in the air and brought it crashing to earth. Fortunately this one, it turned out, could be repaired.

The Baptist Minister's Daughter

In the late 1950s, Dorothy Fosdick was staff director for Senator Henry ("Scoop") Jackson's committee on government operations. Her previous close association with Adlai Stevenson was succeeded by a close relationship with Scoop. Simultaneously, Dorothy moved ideologically on foreign policy from a moderately liberal Stevensonian posture to a hard Cold War Jacksonian one. Jackson harbored a nest of professional anti-Communists, like Richard Perle, who later spearheaded the neo-conservative movement. Fosdick was now a tough girl who believed in a tough foreign policy. Even in the late 1960s, with anti-war protests rocking the nation, Dorothy was still an immovable hawk on Vietnam.

Ironically, she was the daughter of Harry Emerson Fosdick, the famous pacifist minister of the Riverside Church in New York City. In January, 1967, Dorothy was unforgettably featured at All Souls Episcopal Church in Washington. John Sharon, Stevenson's old assistant who had known Dorothy since her Stevenson days, was now a lay reader in the church. He had contrived a kind of reconciliation service for hawks and doves.

In the audience were Clark Clifford, George Ball, and Robert McNamara among other prominent office holders. Adam Yarmolinsky was an usher, and he had been cleverly separating the pro-Vietnam from the anti-Vietnam attendees, seating them on opposite sides of the aisle, like friends of the bride and groom at a wedding.

The now dovish Sharon had carefully arranged the service. It opened with James Russell Lowell's hymn "Once to every man and nation comes the moment to decide—in the strife of truth with falsehood for the good or evil side." But that was only a foretaste of things to come.

Dorothy Fosdick was sitting in the front row with other prominent hawks. Just before Sharon took the pulpit for his dovish sermon, the audience was asked to sing Dorothy's father's stirring hymn, "God of Grace and God of Glory." The opening lines of the second verse began: "Cure Thy children's warring madness. Bend our pride to Thy control." These lines were sung lustily from the dovish pews, with dovish faces all turning in Dorothy's direction.

★ ★ ★

Presidential Requirements in Bonn

Always sensitive about comparisons with his predecessor, LBJ avoided settings where such comparisons would be inevitable. Hence, as President, LBJ avoided Germany and

Berlin in particular. He did, however, go to Bonn and Cologne for Adenauer's funeral in 1967. Despite the solemnity of the occasion, there were the usual elements of LBJ-related farce.

Vice President Humphrey happened to be in Bonn just before, and just after, the Johnson visit. The next time he saw TLH he was still full of what he had heard about the Presidential visit.

After inspecting Ambassador McGhee's residence, the Secret Service had rejected it as an accommodation for LBJ. Considering its proximity to the Rhine, protection from terrorists emerging from the river could not be guaranteed. The inspectors then turned to DCM Martin Hillenbrand's house, which was inside the American diplomatic compound. That seemed safer.

Unfortunately Marty was a great reader, and his bedroom walls were full of books in built-in bookshelves. The LBJ advance team announced that "the President of the United States does not like to wake up in the morning looking at books." So the bedroom windows were darkened with shades, and to make doubly sure, the books themselves were covered to hide the offending views.

Next on official inspection was Hillenbrand's master shower. The shower-head first had to be elevated, more than a foot, to accommodate the Presidential height. The shower's strength also proved inadequate for Presidential needs. "The President of the United States requires needle-point showers." Ultimately a supplementary pump was installed in the basement, and two muscled German attendants hired to be available for instant service. When LBJ indicated that it was shower time, they pumped away ferociously to achieve the semblance of needle-point strength.

It Caught My Eye

While in Bonn, LBJ also focused on the handsome cobalt blue dinner plates that were standard usage in American embassies around the world at the time. For some reason he thought they were of German make and design. "Ah want some for Washington," the President declared. Idar Rimestad, the State Department's administrative officer who accompanied LBJ, was not one to argue with his President or to explain. He quickly commandeered the Pentagon's communication system to reach the Lennox factory back in Ohio.

A large crate of US diplomatic cobalt china was ordered to be flown overnight from Ohio to Bonn/Cologne airport. It was to be assigned the highest priority, to guarantee arrival the next morning alongside Air Force One– no later than 10 a.m. German time, LBJ's scheduled departure time for his return to the US. There exists a photo of LBJ about to climb up the stairs to the Presidential plane, accompanied by a smiling Idar Rimestad pointing proudly to the crate: "And here, Mr. President, is the china that you wanted."

★ ★ ★

Overtaken by Events

In June, 1967, Senator Mondale asked TLH to substitute for him and give a college commencement speech in Bemidji, Minnesota. The Israeli armed forces were on alert that weekend, and Secretary Rusk wanted to know whether the intelligence community thought the Israelis were about to strike. TLH checked around town and told Rusk that the considered wisdom of the community was that the Israelis were ready, but would probably not act quite yet. Embarrassingly, the Six Day War began, just as TLH mounted the platform in Bemidji.

★ ★ ★

Bipartisan Advice between Texans

Once when George H. W. Bush was still a Republican Congressman from Texas, he sought Lyndon Johnson's advice on whether he should run for the Senate in Texas. To Bush's surprise, LBJ said of course he should run. Suspecting an ulterior, probably partisan, motive, Bush asked Johnson to elaborate. "You should try for the United States Senate, George, because the difference between the Senate and the House of Representatives is the difference between chicken salad and chicken shit." Bush ran and lost.

★ ★ ★

The Bush Family Moves Right Along

In Connecticut in 1954, TLH was courting his future wife, Jean Reiman. After graduating from Vassar, she had become a reporter for the New Haven Register. As the newsroom's only Democrat, Jean had been assigned to edit Dorothy Walker Bush's regular column from Washington, where her Republican husband, Prescott Bush, was US Senator. As submitted, Dorothy's column was always two or three times the allowable length, and Jean's job was to cut it and condense. Despite this awkward relationship, Jean grew to admire Dorothy, who at that time was something of a liberal, especially on civil rights. The next generation of Bushes, George and Barbara, had already left Yale and Connecticut, and moved on to Texas to seek their political fortune.

By the early 1970s, George H. W. Bush had become US ambassador to the United Nations. TLH had then become president of the Carnegie Endowment for International Peace, whose headquarters were located across the street from the UN. At lunches with TLH in the delegates' dining room, Bush would explain how vital the UN was to US national security, and how devoted he himself was to expanding its prominence in US foreign policy. Internationalism was the order of the day, as far as Bush was concerned.

By the mid-1970s, George H. W. Bush had gone on to become Chief of the US Liaison Office (putative ambassador) in China. In 1975 at a reception for visiting Americans given by the Bushes at their residence in Beijing, he explained that he wasn't all that busy, since there were as yet no official relations. TLH mentioned that the Bush family, anyway, probably enjoyed visiting China. Whereupon Barbara Bush said: "Our son Neil enjoys coming, and even little Jeb enjoys it. But of course, our son George W. is not interested in foreign affairs. He is into baseball."

Resigning to Run for President

In 1977 George H. W. Bush attended a Trilateral Commission meeting in Bonn, Germany. He was about to emerge from Texas into presidential politics. Sitting alone at breakfast one morning, he motioned for TLH to join him. "You know,

Tom, I am going to have to resign from organizations like this one and the Council on Foreign Relations. They are much too internationalist for many of my friends. I have trouble explaining my membership. A lot of my friends just don't understand it—they just don't accept it."

At that point David Rockefeller suddenly joined us. The Trilateral Commission and the Council on Foreign Relations were perhaps identified with him more than anyone else. TLH said: "David, George has been telling me that he is going to have to resign from both the Commission and the Council because his friends don't understand his belonging to such groups." Rockefeller looked crestfallen. "But George, I thought WE were your friends!"

Once he became President, however, George H. W. Bush, resuscitated many of his old relationships. After his return from the Malta summit with Gorbachev, for example, he invited TLH to a private de-briefing at the White House.

An Ephemeral Promotion

In December, 1964, shortly after the Johnson-Humphrey election victory, LBJ met at his Texas ranch with Dean Rusk, McGeorge Bundy, and Bill Moyers. At lunch with TLH a week later, Moyers asked if TLH had heard about the meeting. He had not.

According to Moyers, the principal subject on the agenda was filling the State Department vacancy caused by the departure of U. Alexis Johnson to become deputy ambassador in Saigon. The job he had held was Deputy Under Secretary for Political Affairs, the key State position between the geographical bureaus and the Secretary. It had become a critical link in the hierarchy of influence on Vietnam. That spot had traditionally been a position reserved for the career foreign service, but Rusk, usually devoted to the foreign service, now proposed TLH for the post.

The President and Bundy voiced their consent, and TLH's appointment was agreed to. The meeting went on to other subjects. Suddenly Rusk said, "On second thought, I'd like to withdraw my suggestion that Tom Hughes take Alex Johnson's job. Let's sleep on it." Without further explanation, the matter was taken off the table. Rusk never explained his change of mind. Nobody else had an explanation either, and TLH never raised the matter with Rusk. Moyers said that both Bundy and Johnson remained perplexed over Rusk's behavior.

Had TLH been promoted to the Deputy Under Secretary position, he would have been a key link in the policy chain of command and would have been in a position to strengthen George Ball in his recalcitrance over Vietnam. One of the arguably admirable characteristics of Dean Rusk was his willingness, over eight years in office, to suffer three Under Secretaries in a row–Bowles, Ball, and Katzenbach–who steadily questioned his whole Vietnam project. TLH would have bolstered that opposition.

Shortly after the meeting at the ranch, Rusk selected TLH as the State Department's nominee for the Arthur Flemming award for distinguished young men in government. The nominating letter from Ambassador Llwellyn Thompson concluded: "For intellectual power, executive skill, versatility, and unfailing zest and good humor, I would rate him A+

with several oak leaf clusters for extraordinary performance." Confronted with such heights of hyperbole, the awards committee had little recourse. TLH shared the Flemming prize in February, 1965, with Pat Moynihan and Paul Volcker.

Top Secret in the Afterlife

The Raborn regime was mercifully brief at CIA, and its chief beneficiary was Richard Helms, a career officer who became Raborn's deputy and, before long, his successor. Two decades later TLH had a phone call from the CIA saying that they were putting together a collective biography of CIA's many directors. TLH must have known the early ones–Dulles, McCone, Raborn, Helms, et al– and they would like to interview him for their book. TLH agreed.

On arrival, the interrogator put a recording device on the table and said: "I'm going to record this, if you have no objection." "I have no objection, but I would like a copy of it please, if you don't mind." "A COPY! But it will all be classified!" "Classified? At what point does it become classified?" "As soon as you start to speak." "Now this is really rather amusing, don't you think? You will try, won't you, to get me a copy of the remarks I am about to make." "Yes, but I am not optimistic." "All right. You've come a long way. Let's proceed. But please use your best efforts to get me a copy?" "If you insist, I'll try, but I can't promise a thing."

Afterwards TLH received an official letter from the CIA saying that the interview had "opened vistas" and was very helpful in their biographical project. Unfortunately, as they had suspected, the interview was almost entirely classified. Perhaps there were a few bits that TLH might be able to read some day if he wanted to come out to Langley.

Soon afterwards, TLH saw Richard Helms at a cocktail party and told him about his CIA interview. "Unfortunately, Dick, you'll never be able to read the nice things I said about you, because it's classified and you have no 'need to know'."

★ ★ ★

Spoiling a White House Briefing

One morning in August, 1966, Dean Rusk summoned TLH to his office to tell him that the White House, at the noon briefing, was going to announce his appointment as Assistant Secretary of State for the Near East and South Asia. "Gosh, nobody has talked to me about this." "Oh, is there some reason you would not like to move to NEA?" "Well, for starters I am very happy where I am. Second, I was once a kibbutznik in Israel, which would not endear me to many Arab governments. And third, I have twice worked for Chester Bowles, and that connection would not endear me to the Pakistanis. Thanks for the offer but, on quick reflection, I think I would prefer to remain where I am."

TLH's friend David Ginsburg was sitting in Rusk's outer office as TLH left. Coincidentally TLH was having lunch with Ginsburg that same day, and they later compared notes on their meetings. Rusk told Ginsburg that at the White House noon briefing his appointment to the Number 3 position, the State Department's Undersecretary for Economic Affairs, was going to be announced.

Ginsburg said that was a great honor, but who would the new Undersecretary be, with whom he would have to work?

Rusk said he was not at liberty to disclose the name, but it would be a patriotic American with whom Ginsburg would have no problem, he was sure. Ginsburg then said, "Well, I'm sorry, if you can't tell me who the Undersecretary will be, I'm afraid I will have to decline." So there were now two prospective appointees who would not be announced at the White House noon briefing.

Eugene Rostow, the Dean of Yale School, who had been waiting for years to be summoned back to Washington, was then called and offered the Number 3 position instead of Ginsburg. He asked the same question about the identity of the Undersecretary, and got the same answer—a patriotic American whose name Rusk was not at liberty to disclose. Unlike Ginsburg, Rostow nevertheless accepted, only to learn at the noon briefing that the new Undersecretary would be Nick Katzenbach, with whom he had a difficult relationship, to put it mildly, on the Yale Law School faculty in the 1950s. The two men awkwardly occupied opposite ends of the State Department's seventh floor for the last year-and-a-half of the Johnson administration.

After McNamara's chief adviser, John McNaughton, was killed in an air crash in July, 1967, TLH was sounded out by White House head-hunter Lloyd Cutler as John's possible successor at the Pentagon. Once again, TLH declined, preferring to stay in INR.

LBJ Torments His VP on Vietnam

By 1967, Vice President Humphrey was supposedly back in President Johnson's good graces with his public embrace of the

Vietnam War. But their relationship remained delicate. Just how delicate, TLH learned one morning when HHH drove him to work in his official limousine, with Secret Service cars preceding and following it.

Humphrey stopped the procession in Rock Creek Park, got out of his limousine, and said: "Let's jog down the pathway here," ahead of the Secret Service and their walkie-talkies. Humphrey then said, rather off-handedly: "You know, Tom, this is the only time during the day that I am not being listened to." (The Vice President knew he was being taped by the President. Robert Dallek's book on LBJ tells how much Johnson loved to listen to Humphrey's phone conversations.)

TLH said something like, "Apart from that, my friend, what else is new?" "Well, as you know, Muriel and I are leaving Chevy Chase to move into our new apartment at Harbor Square, nearer the Capitol. We had a little house-warming there last night, and Lyndon and Lady Bird joined us as our first guests." "Oh, that must have been quite a family reunion." "Yeah, you can say that again."

"Lyndon stretched right out on my new sofa, started scratching himself, and said: "Now Hubert. Ah understand you make the best speeches on Vietnam of anyone in the entire administration. The President can't leave the White House without facing storms of student protests. The Secretary of Defense gets stoned at Harvard. But it's different with the Vice President. Everyone says that you make the best speech on Vietnam. Ah want to hear it."

Getting increasingly uncomfortable, Humphrey murmured: "Oh, I just try to make the usual points." "No, Ah don't want to hear the points, Hubert, Ah want to hear the speech." So the captive Vice President is about to declaim on demand, right there in his new living room. Then Johnson gets up to go to the bathroom, saying: "Keep talkin', Hubert, Ah'm listnin." Lady Bird and Muriel had fortunately finished their preparations in the kitchen. The steaks were ready just in time.

RFK Informs LBJ

Harry McPherson, counsel to LBJ, had an entertaining inside account of Bobby Kennedy's confrontation with LBJ in the 1968 presidential sweepstakes. Before his public announcement, Bobby made an appointment to tell LBJ that he planned to run against him. Lyndon took Bobby into the room at the White House with the tape recorder and turned it on. Led on by LBJ, Bobby said one thing after another that LBJ thought would be hugely embarrassing to Bobby in his forthcoming campaign. Johnson couldn't believe his good luck in having it all on tape.

As soon as Kennedy left, Lyndon eagerly asked for the transcript. A few minutes later, his assistant came back looking crestfallen. "Mr. President, I'm sorry. There's nothing on the tape but a whirling sound." Bobby had brought a scrambler along and wrecked the precious recording.

When he finally achieved his lifelong dream of becoming the Democratic nominee for President in 1968, Hubert Humphrey found himself in the identical predicament that Adlai Stevenson had faced in 1952: the dilemma of how to champion the Democratic party, without embracing an unpopular Democratic president and an unpopular war.

American public patience for Vietnam had run out–just
as Humphrey's memo to Johnson in February, 1965, had
predicted —and just as public patience for Korea had run out
for Stevenson and Truman in 1952.

IV

IN LONDON WITH ANNENBERG
★ ★ ★

The Nixon-Kissinger Takeover

TLH had accompanied Dean Rusk on a visit to Germany in May, 1962. One night in Bonn, Chancellor Konrad Adenauer, then in his upper eighties, hosted a Herrenabend (stag dinner) for Rusk at the Palais Schaumburg. Afterwards, over brandy, Adenauer discovered that TLH was responsible for analysis and research in the State Department. He inquired how we kept in touch with the academic world in general and with Professor Henry Kissinger of Harvard in particular. Adenauer allowed as how Kissinger was the most compelling academic mind he had come across in his many decades of public service. "If he had only remained a German, he might well have become Chancellor—after me, of course," said der Alte.

★ ★ ★

An Available Genius

During the Nixon-Humphrey presidential contest in 1968, Kissinger managed to convince both campaigns of his support.

He angled his advice to both candidates cleverly enough, so that he was a serious candidate for national security adviser, no matter who won.

He explicitly foresaw his own impact on the State Department bureaucracy by writing at the time: "The impact of genius on institutions is bound to be unsettling…The bureaucrat will consider originality as unsafe, and the genius will resent the constriction of routine…To force genius to respect norms may be chafing, but to encourage mediocrity to imitate greatness may produce institutionalized hysteria…"

★ ★ ★

Unexpected Developments in London

Following Humphrey's defeat by Nixon in 1968, TLH was asked by Brookings President Kermit Gordon to join him there as Vice President. Meanwhile, until his successor at INR was chosen, TLH stayed at the State Department. He began jointly briefing the new Secretary, William P. Rogers, and his deputy, Elliot Richardson. It quickly became evident that they had different attention spans—say five minutes for Rogers, and a half-hour or so for Richardson. "If you want to persist in all this, Elliot, you can do it on your own time." So TLH began briefing them separately, while maintaining friendly relations with both.

Meanwhile, in London, the BBC produced its film called "Royal Family." It focused on Ambassador Annenberg's arrival at Buckingham Palace to present his credentials to the Queen. In an episode immortalized in technicolor, he hesitantly entered the palace, nearly forgot to take off his top hat, and was instructed by Sir Denis Greenhill on how to present his credentials. "We take one pace forward with our left foot, and then make a little bow during the hand-shaking."

Once face to face, the Queen pleasantly inquired about the Annenbergs' housing arrangements—were they now in Winfield House, or still making-do at Claridge's? Annenberg then spoke his famous lines: "We are in the ambassadorial residence, subject, of course, to some of the discomfiture as a result of the need for elements of refurbishing and rehabilitation."

The Queen's encounter with the American ambassador promptly set Broadcast House and Fleet Street into uproars of mirth: "Lost in his polysyllables." "Early Chaplin." "Genuine American folk-Baroque." "The greatest sentence since Beowulf."

★ ★ ★

A Job Reassessment

Back in Washington, weeks and months had passed with no successor for TLH in INR. TLH told Rogers that Brookings was becoming impatient. Would they please find a successor, so that he could comfortably leave? " "But why would anyone want to go to Brookings anyway?" Rogers asked. "I've got a better idea. Our new ambassador in Britain needs a good deputy. How about going over to London and helping us out?"

"You've got to be kidding. You must know of my Democratic affiliations, including my long-time association with the loser in the recent election." "Humphrey? Oh, Hubert's a swell guy." "Be that as it may, I doubt that I would be considered a plausible DCM in London by either the Foreign Service or the Republican party." "But they have a Labour government over there," Rogers went on, "and we understand that you once worked for the Senate Labor Committee." "Until now, I'd never made that connection." "Well, please consider it seriously. Elliot and I think you're the right man to help Ambassador Annenberg. "

The Hughes Crisis

After a week's reflection, TLH decided the offer was too enticing to turn down. There was a luncheon for Annenberg at Blair House, where TLH was announced as his new deputy. Politicians of both parties in Washington were astonished, and there were outcries from Republicans in the society columns. The foreign service was also unhappy at being deprived of a choice post. Otherwise everything seemed smooth sailing, and the Hughes family prepared to leave for England.

Years later, in 2008, when Henry Kissinger's telephone calls became public at the National Archives, it was disclosed that the appointment had stoked a hornet's nest at the White House. Nixon went through the roof and told Kissinger to stop the whole transaction. Henry phoned Richardson to tell him "Hughes is not going to London." "But it's all arranged. The British are happy, Annenberg is happy, and the Hugheses are packing their bags."

"Well, stop it. He's not going. We need a loyal man there. There must be a security problem." "No, the security people have checked Hughes out, and they find nothing adverse." "The President won't sign anything." "He doesn't have to. It's not a Presidential appointment." Exasperated, Kissinger concludes: "There will be a meeting at the White House this afternoon at three p.m.—with the President, Rogers, me, and you."

Also attending was Richard Allen, another Nixon advisor. He later told TLH that the "meeting on the Hughes crisis" was memorable, but he was saving the juicy details for his own memoirs. Apparently the crisis had innocently provided early ammunition for the incipient internecine struggle between Nixon and Kissinger, on the one hand, and Rogers and Richardson on the other. At minimum it nicely fed into Kissinger's game plan to nudge Rogers aside, eventually unseating and succeeding him, while running foreign policy from the White House in the meantime.

A Tutor Recollects

An Oxford don, who had a vague recollection of TLH from 1947-9, happened to be visiting Washington at the time of the Hughes crisis. When reminded that he might have tutored TLH twenty years earlier, and told of the eminence of his forthcoming position in London, the don responded: "Oh, yes, him. I say. He's done disappointingly well."

A Matter of Presidential Importance

A couple of months later, the tapes revealed another phone call, this one from Kissinger to Annenberg in London. "You should know, Walter, that the President still has a watchful eye on Tom Hughes." "Oh, everything is going along smoothly. No problems. Tom is very supportive." "Well, if anything untoward should happen, you will want to report it immediately." "Oh, if anything untoward should happen, I would call you at once." "Oh, no Walter, on a matter of this importance, you don't call me. You call the President direct."

Advance Notices

As TLH, the newly minted diplomat, set sail with his family for England in September, 1969, the media coverage on both sides of the Atlantic continued full throttle. The Guardian commented helpfully: "Unlike his Ambassador, Mr. Hughes has a wide knowledge of foreign affairs and government as an Assistant Secretary of State. He employs the English language with a felicity granted to distressingly few Americans."

Ben Welles at the Pentagon sent the following message to be delivered at the embassy on arrival: "My friend and journalistic colleague, Peter Grosse, is writing a story in which he mentions you as follows: 'Thomas L. Hughes, a brilliant ex-Democratic political activist, will be putting Ambassador Walter Annenberg on and off the diplomatic potty when he gets to London.'"

Replacing Presidential Photos

Responsibilities at the London embassy began in earnest. At the morning staff meeting, the administrative section announced that five dozen photographs of a frowning President Nixon had arrived for display in all embassy offices.

For the past two weeks, often with limited enthusiasm, embassy personnel had been busy putting them in place. Suddenly Washington cabled that the frowning images had been deemed unsuitable for display and should be destroyed. They were replaced by five dozen photos of a smiling Nixon that soon arrived by Pan American overnight express.

Warm Receptions

The Annenbergs outdid themselves welcoming TLH and Jean. First there was an intimate dinner for the ranking embassy staff held at Annabel's, then the rage of London restaurants. This was followed by a celebrity reception at Claridge's to enable luminaries to be announced like "Mr. Rudolph Nureyev," "Madame Margo Fontaine," and "Mr. Francis Sinatra" to meet the embassy's new arrivals. (Earlier that day the Court Circular in the Times had said: "King Hussein has returned to Claridge's after visit to Amman.")

The ambassador invited a dozen or so British industrialists, along with some ranking Conservative politicians to meet TLH for "a behind-the-scenes discussion" at the Dorchester. At Thanksgiving, after reading the scripture at the American Church, TLH addressed the American Society in London. The British reciprocated as well, and Sir Denis Greenhill hosted a lavish affair at Lancaster House for TLH to meet with and speak to the Foreign Office bureaucracy.

At the annual reception by the Queen at Buckingham Palace, however, the three ranking American diplomatic wives displayed certain protocolary contrasts. As Her Majesty approached, Mrs. Annenberg executed an elaborate and well-practiced, curtsey. Mrs. Hughes, the next in line, extended her hand to the queen. After that, Mrs. Cleveland offered a little bow that was distinct but short.

Honoring One's Predecessor

Ambassador Annenberg took his responsibility seriously as the "ambassador of all Americans." He understandably detested one of his predecessors, Joseph P. Kennedy. "That miserable rat" died soon after Annenberg reached London. Walter nevertheless generously ordered a memorial book to be placed with the marine guards at the Embassy entrance, so that any mourners of Joe Kennedy could sign. Each page was headed "the week of…the week of…"

At each subsequent weekly staff meeting, Annenberg routinely inquired about the signatures of condolence. He seemed gratified when informed that there had been none so far. Finally after six weeks had elapsed, two Irishmen visiting from Boston appeared and signed the book. Annenberg then said, rather triumphantly, "Good. Let's close the book now, and send it to the family for auld lang syne." It took some imaginative staff subterfuge to avoid following these instructions.

The Picture Hanging Ceremony.

In October, 1969, the Annenbergs' glorious French impressionist paintings arrived in London to be displayed in the refurbished embassy residence. Although Scotland Yard explained that they had been hanging pictures in London for several centuries, the ambassador was determined that only the FBI could be entrusted with the task. After a personal approach to his friend, J. Edgar Hoover, six FBI agents were dispatched to London. They arrived at Winfield House, the embassy residence, just as Walter and Lee took off for Baden-Baden for a few days of rest.

In their absence, TLH was in charge. It fell to him to supervise the G-men, for whom Cezanne landscapes and Monet water lilies were a totally new and unfamiliar experience. They struggled to hoist each precious painting onto its assigned place, taking care not to damage unnecessarily the handsome antique green Chinese wallpaper that had laboriously just been rescued from a baronial house in Ireland.

An Arrest in the Kitchen

As the morning progressed, TLH wandered into the kitchen where, astonishingly, he found the chief chef of the Belgian embassy and the deputy chef of the American embassy busy divvying up hundred pound notes at the kitchen table. Lee Annenberg had already decided to promote the American deputy chef to become her chief chef, after some further professional training at the Cordon Bleu in Paris.

Through the kitchen window, a van with steaming caviar could be seen, parked in the courtyard. It looked suspiciously like something nefarious might be going on. TLH returned to the living room to tell the chief FBI picture-hanger that he might want to visit the kitchen. This was American property after all, where arrests could be made. Crime detection was more his line of work anyway. He was thrilled to take on a more congenial assignment, and, upon inspection, he apprehended the culprits. TLH had the bittersweet task of calling the Brenner's Park Hotel in Baden-Baden to inform lively Lee that her prospective chef would probably not be going to the Cordon Bleu after all, but was about to be turned over to the custody of the British police.

The Losers come to Dinner

One morning in the autumn of 1969, Ambassador Annenberg excitedly came into TLH's embassy office and announced that "the Romneys are coming." This was the former Republican governor of Michigan, George Romney, who had run unsuccessfully for the Presidential nomination a year earlier. During his campaign he had confessed that military briefers had "brainwashed" him in Vietnam, and that had contributed to his defeat.

"Lee and I don't entertain losers," Annenberg explained. "You and Jean have a dinner for him." So we did, on September 26. The protocol office had struggled for a week to find some British guests who would like to attend a dinner at Wychwood House for the Romneys. They finally came up with some minor ministers.

Just as the group was about to sit down for dinner, there was a knock on the front door. Who should be there but Eugene McCarthy. He said: "Oh, you are having a dinner party. I'll join you." We said maybe that was not such a good idea. The guest of honor might not relish McCarthy's company, and vice versa. "You mean you are having a dinner for Romney from Michigan, the one who was brainwashed?" "Yes, the very one." "I always thought," said McCarthy, "that a light rinse would have been enough." "Well, anyway, that's probably enough from you, Gene. Your bedroom is on the third floor. We'll tell you all about it in the morning."

"And Now my Assistant will Explain"

On the rare occasions when the ambassador was summoned to the British foreign office to explain some controversial American policy, he would ask his DCM to accompany him. In one such incident, Sir Alex Douglas-Hume, then Foreign Secretary, was perplexed about the US rationale for supplying yet another squadron of fighter aircraft to the Israelis. After some initial pleasantries, Annenberg bowed out by saying: "And now, to answer your questions. I have brought along my assistant, Mr. Hughes. You may put your questions to him directly."

Codel: Meet Me at Southampton

The American Embassy in London had long been a favorite stop for members of Congress. Congressional delegations

("Codels") invariably found it necessary to visit London first, no matter where in Europe their official destination might be. Joan Auten was the all-purpose Embassy staffer dedicated to Congressional service. For instance, she was personally assigned to hand out the "soft currency" to Ohio Congressman Wayne Hayes for his antiques shopping sprees.

The terror of the State Department in the 60s, however, was the House Appropriations Committee chairman, John Rooney. He was always met at Southampton, when his ship arrived. The embassy's chief administrative officer invariably handled this assignment in person. At embassy staff meetings, there were occasional suggestions that notices should be posted at Heathrow Airport: "Attention Congressmen. FYI. It is unnecessary to travel into metropolitan London if you are scheduled for Paris or Rome. You can save both time and energy by flying onward directly from this airport." Like so many good ideas…

★ ★ ★

First Things First

Meanwhile the trans-Atlantic circuits remained lively. In Washington, Art Buchwald penned a column entitled "What If They Kidnapped Annenberg?" Embassy life in London was equally serious. Admiral Kirn was our ranking Naval Person. By sheer coincidence, he and the ambassador happened to have been classmates at the Peddie School—"birds of a feather, Tom, birds of a feather!" So no one expected a major dispute. Their old school tie, however, soon proved insufficient.

The struggle for parking at the embassy was acute. The spaces allotted to genuine diplomats had been squeezed over the years, and they now accounted for only about 30 percent of the total. The ambassador's personal amanuensis from Philadelphia, Robert Montgomery Scott, was destined to be the most indispensable man in the embassy. It was clearly essential for him to park, and therefore a single parking space had to be taken away from those previously allotted. Straws were drawn among the host of competing agencies who enjoyed parking privileges—Agriculture, Commerce, Labor, and Treasury; Defense, Army, Navy, and Air Force; not to mention the assorted secret unmentionables. Unfortunately for the Navy, it lost in the draw.

Not accustomed to losing, Admiral Kirn cast aside all Peddie School attachments and immediately boarded a plane for Washington to take the matter up with the Pentagon. The navy's threatened loss of a parking space in the London embassy clearly merited urgent reconsideration, at least at the level of the Joint Chiefs of Staff. The strife was considerable, but ultimately the navy had to give way. Afterwards the fraternal relations between the two classmates were never quite the same.

The Mayflower: On Second Thought

In 1970 there was an important anniversary–the voyage of the Mayflower and the arrival of the Pilgrims in America. As a Mayflower descendant, TLH was asked to deliver a speech representing the embassy at the festivities in Plymouth. To commemorate the historic event itself, the Embassy bureaucracy had prepared a handsomely printed document for presentation at the ceremony.

Reading it over on the train to Devon, TLH was astonished that it rhapsodized about "this 300th anniversary." For once the American Minister was emboldened to correct his bureaucratic underlings. Surely the Pilgrims had sailed in 1620, not 1670. The printed documents with the embarrassing error were quietly consigned to the dustbins en route, and the speaker was able, rather ingloriously, to announce that appropriate documents would soon be sent to Plymouth in honor of the 350th anniversary.

★ ★ ★

A Fleur Cowles Reception

The arrival in London of Walter Lippmann was the occasion for an elaborate feast in his honor, given by his friend, the ranking American socialite, Fleur Cowles. The A-list of invitees, including Ambassador Annenberg, assembled for dinner in her quarters at the Albany. The B-list of invitees including TLH—the second tranche– were invited for coffee around 10 p.m. after the others had dined.

On arrival, TLH found the guest of honor sitting, rather red-faced, under a potted palm at the entrance. Lippmann said: "We're on our way out, Tom! It was a disaster. You'll hear all about it. Now we all know what you have to put up with everyday. Thank God you're here! Goodnight!" In the inner sanctum, Annenberg looked equally flustered. "He didn't even say goodbye," the ambassador complained about Lippmann.

Other guests soon disclosed what had happened. At one end of Fleur's table, Annenberg had begun discoursing negatively about General de Gaulle, with whom he had had a longtime feud, probably unknown to the general. The ambassador accused the French president of all kinds of perfidy—recognizing Communist China, opposing the US war in Vietnam, weakening NATO, and trying to seduce the West Germans away from their American allies.

Annenberg seemed quite unaware of Lippmann's well known sympathy for de Gaulle. Finally the guest of honor could stand it no longer. "Fleur, you do give the best parties in London. But this one has been spoiled by this so-called ambassador of ours, whom you have felt obliged to invite. I'm sorry, but I can't continue to sit here and listen to him spout all this nonsense. He's an embarrassment to our country, and as soon as everyone realizes it, the better. We're leaving."

The Guildhall Banquet

The annual banquet of the Lord Mayor of London took place at the Guildhall in late 1969. In the Annenbergs' absence, TLH in white tie and tails, and Jean in equally suitable finery, were announced by trumpeters at the entrance. As they proceeded down the main aisle, the musicians struck up the Star Spangled Banner. Eventually they took their place near the little platform where Prime Minister Harold Wilson sat with the Lord Mayor, waving to their friends.

At the banquet itself, TLH and Jean sat across from a beribboned Air Vice Marshal and his wife. Early on, the Air Marshal's monocle fell into his soup, splashing it disconcertingly onto his ribbons. Jean then tried to divert attention from the mishap by saying she had been busy "dropping cards" on other embassy wives. But this only reminded Mrs. Air Vice Marshal of "rhino droppings." She was referring to Henry Moore's reclining sculptures at the Tate. She said she understood that Ambassador Annenberg liked that kind of thing. "If so, would he please find some way to take these rhino droppings away, and deposit them somewhere in America, where they would be appreciated? I'll leave the matter in your own good hands."

Just then, Harold Wilson took the floor to praise his government for having completed an entire year with no armed forces fatalities. "I am especially proud to say that during the past twelve months, not a single British soldier has lost his life in the nation's service." "FOR SHAME, Prime Minister!" shouted the Air Vice Marshal's wife. "FOR SHAME!"

Another Memorable Phrase

The ambasador's florid phraseology continued to entertain an attentive British audience. One day he reportedly met Nicholas Soames, Churchill's grandson, and told him: "Mr. Soames, I have had the honor of meeting your mother last week. I must say, she is a rose plucked from the herbaceous border of British motherhood." To which Soames reportedly replied: "Yes, she is, rather…isn't she?"

Lauren Bacall's Oxford Friend

High tables at Oxford were also amused after hearing about Lauren Bacall, sitting next to an Englishman at dinner in Paris. She asked him where he lived. "Oxford" he replied.

"Then perhaps you know my closest, dearest, Oxford friend, Professor Isaiah Berlin?" Her dinner partner replied: "I am he."

On British Statesmen

Lord George-Brown, Foreign Minister in the Labour government on his colleagues: "Most British statesmen have either drunk too much or womanized too much. I never fell into the second category."

Safely into Port

In 1969 the Hughes family lived at Cottesmore Gardens in Kensington, directly across the street from the house where Princess Margaret's assignations with Captain Townsend had famously occurred, some years before. In her tempestuous career, her oscillations from lovers to husband to lovers, were amplified by her fondness for drink. Upon her death, one obituary writer wrote for many: "We all thought affectionately of our dear Princess Margaret, and we suffered with her through her many afflictions. It was a relief to learn that, toward the end, she had come safely into port."

The Lure of Rancho Mirage

One Friday afternoon Kissinger called TLH in London. "Tom, this is a non-conversation." "Of course, Henry, all of your conversations are non-conversations. What is it this time?"

"It's about Palm Springs. This weekend. Ve might go, but vould they come?" Nixon and Kissinger liked Sunnylands, the Annenberg's palatial residential complex at Rancho Mirage, California, especially if the Annenbergs weren't there. "No, Henry, there's no way the jet-star can be turned around and get to California this weekend. They're already unpacking in Baden-Baden. "Good, ve vill go."

Other Photos of Interest

The Duchess of Argyle's adultery trial in Edinburgh was that season's object of intense prurient entertainment. Groups from London would embark on overnight trips to Scotland to attend the judicial proceedings. The aging Duke of Argyle had arranged to have compromising photographs taken of his wife in flagrante delicto. The spectators' attention in the courtroom was riveted on the bedroom photos of the naked rear ends of her paramours.

There were two leading suspects—a professional Anglophile, Douglas Fairbanks, Jr., and the German Ambassador, Sigismund von Braun. Dinner parties in London intensely debated the philanderer's identity. One lady of experience would say: "It's got to be Siggy von Braun. It's distinctively Siggy. No question about it." Her social rival would be equally adamant: "Nonsense. Of course it's Duggie Fairbanks. I ought to know. It's certainly Duggie. There can be no doubt."

Nixon's Palace Guard

Buckingham Palace was thrilling for the Annenbergs, and they often lamented privately over the contrast with the inadequate rituals in Washington. Trying to compensate, in the spring of 1970, Nixon proudly dressed up his White House flunkies in Viennese operatic uniforms. This Nixonian pretentiousness deeply offended the seriously stylish Lee Annenberg, "It's light opera right now at the White House, just like the Merry Widow." Years later, Lee became Reagan's Chief of Protocol.

The Reagans Arrive

The London visit of Governor and Mrs. Ronald Reagan was a relief for the Annenbergs. As between the two sets of Californians—the Nixons and the Reagans—it was clear whom they preferred. For years the Reagans spent every New Year's eve with the Annenbergs at Rancho Mirage.

The ambassador told TLH that the Reagans really didn't know what they were going to do, when his term as governor expired. Nancy was falling in love with London, especially with the gentry and the royals. This led to embassy corridor discussion about the possibility that the Reagans might leave politics and move to Britain. The ambassador, indeed, had this contingency in mind, and he explored finding a fashionable apartment for them in the Albany where they could live near Fleur Cowles and Ted Heath. In fact, Annenberg made it clear that he would gladly "contribute the necessary where-with-all" to facilitate this happy landing.

A Weekend in Brussels

The ambassador then asked TLH whether he and Jean wouldn't like to join them for a weekend in Brussels. "There will just be the six of us—the Reagans, the Annenbergs, and the Hugheses. We'll stay at the embassy there with the John Eisenhowers." It was no sooner said than done.

In Belgium on Saturday morning, Reagan came down in his kimono and slippers, obviously hoping for a quiet day at the embassy residence. Nancy, by contrast, was dressed for high adventure. She turned to lively Lee Annenberg asking: "And what's on the schedule today, Lee?" Lee quickly replied: "I was thinking diamonds." "Diamonds? Antwerp? Chauffeur?" All that was possible, and off "the girls" went. Towards evening they returned with smiles on their faces, after an apparently successful day of diamond hunting.

Meanwhile Reagan himself had been reminiscing about his youth in Dixon, Illinois, which had "shaped my mind for all the years to come." He said he had "enjoyed every whizzing moment of it–sitting in the local theater, watching the flickering antics of Tom Mix and William S. Hart as they foiled robbers and villains, and escorted beautiful girls to safety, waving back from their horses as they cantered into the sunset." Reagan added that he was astonished to read that Shirley Temple was now forty-one years old. "It seems like only yesterday that we were child stars together."

Schmidt Recalls a Summit

One night in Hamburg some years later, former German Chancellor Helmut Schmidt was happily recalling his "summit" with then President Reagan at Williamsburg, Virginia. "I think Giscard and I were supposed to teach him economics." Jim Baker had showed Reagan his thick briefing book, placed at his bedside in the Williamsburg Inn. Baker told the President that he would probably want to read it in some detail before meeting with his French and German visitors the next day.

Later Schmidt heard that the following morning Baker noticed that the briefing book seemed undisturbed from where he had left it the night before. When he asked the President whether he had any questions based on his briefing material, Reagan responded: "Oh, I never opened it. You see, last night they were showing 'The Sound of Music'."

Annenberg's Newspaper World

As if he were clairvoyant, anticipating the Watergate crisis yet to come, Nixon made an attempt to interest Annenberg in buying the Washington Post. He talked to Walter about it, but neither of them was really sure that Kay Graham's family stake in the Post was purchasable.

As the owner of TV Guide, Racing Form, and the Philadelphia Inquirer, however, newspapers were always uppermost in Annenberg's view of the business world. He told TLH one morning that there would soon be front page press attention over his prospective sale of the Philadelphia Inquirer, and he wanted TLH to be "forewarned." When the great day came, however, one of Annenberg's sisters upstaged him on the front pages, with her gift of a fabulous diamond to the Smithsonian.

A Little Dividend

When British guests finished dining amid the Monet water lilies in the Winfield House dining room, the men would adjourn to the living room sofas. When TLH emerged to join them, Annenberg would say: "Shoo-oot your way in, Uncle Tom. Shoo-oot your way in, as my father used to say." Then the butler would arrive with the port or brandy, and the ambassador would ask his guests: "How about a little div-i-dend?"

Moses Annenberg, Walter's father, had been found guilty of tax evasion in a Racing Form scandal in the late1930s. His plea bargaining with the Justice Department had kept Walter off the indictment in return for Moses going to jail. Consequently Walter had a tender spot for his father. Indeed French painters were commissioned to paint the father behind bars in jail. Some of the resulting portraits could be found on the walls of the ambassador's office. They had discrete little bars in the lower left corners to indicate the period of their composition, as well as captions below that read: "Let everything one does in one's life be to one's father's memory."

A Diplomatic Donor at Work

Annenberg worked hard to ingratiate himself with the British public. His largesse was liberally dispensed, countrywide. The American Textile Museum in Bath was handsomely subsidized. Cathedrals in Britain were given chalices engraved "In Memory of the Ambassadorship of Walter H. Annenberg." A photographer he discovered in Vienna was brought to London to photograph Westminster Abbey, resulting in a handsome volume with articles by professionals, including Sir Kenneth Clark.

There was also the Annenberg subsidy for a bi-partisan swimming pool at Chequers, "open to both Conservative and Labour prime ministers on a non-partisan basis." After visiting the Inner Temple in London and discovering the sword of Sir Francis Drake, the ambassador promptly ordered a copy of the sword made for Lincoln's Inn, whose lawyers, although bewildered, cheerfully accepted the gift.

A New DCM Found Wanting

When TLH left London and the Annenbergs, he was succeeded as minister by Jerry Greene who coincidentally had been number two for Chester Bowles earlier in India. He quickly got into trouble by unsuccessfully asserting his rank over Bill Galloway, Annenberg's conservative protégé, who headed the embassy's political section. Greene was unceremoniously dismissed by Annenberg and he landed in Cairo as charge'.

Shortly thereafter, Golda Meir came to London from Israel. She stopped by the embassy to see if she could induce the ambassador to increase his annual contribution to United Jewish Appeal. At first he held firm to his normal donation limit, until an idea suddenly struck him. "Golda, I'll –g-give you another million if you will do one thing for me. B-bomb the American embassy in Cairo. That's where Mr. G–greene has gone."

Back at Rancho Mirage

After surrendering his embassy and returning to Rancho Mirage, Annenberg resumed one of his stranger practices. He would take instant umbrage over someone, often someone he had never met. To indicate his displeasure, he would order signs posted at the entrance of his private Rancho Mirage golf course. For example, one of them began: "The following Hollywood starlets are forbidden to play on this course."

There was one celebrity, however, who was never in danger of being proscribed. One day Annenberg took the time, after a leisurely golf game, to write about him to TLH: "Dear Uncle Tom: Here I am at my nineteenth hole with the Prince of Wales. He is writing to his wife, and I am writing to you."

"Take a Note of It"

In 1981 the Prince of Wales, came to Washington to speak at the annual Oxford-Cambridge dinner. TLH had last met him at the independence celebrations in the Bahamas. Now, at pre-dinner cocktails, the planning committee lined up to exchange a word or two with the prince.

Once vis-à-vis, Charles told TLH that he had "just come from Australia, where I heard the most terrible things about this man Murdoch. I can't tell you what awful things I heard about him. Rupert Murdoch. Here he is, taking over The Times, the only newspaper I have ever read. What would you do, Mr. Hughes, if you were in my situation?"

Grasping for a straw, TLH replied: "Well, Your Royal Highness, there is always the International Herald Tribune." "The what?" he asked. "The International Herald Tribune. It's printed in Paris, and gives you highlights from the New York Times and the Washington Post. I'm sure they will be happy to deliver a copy to Buckingham Palace, if you subscribe." The heir-apparent to the throne beckoned to his aide-de-camp, saying: "Take a note of it! International Herald Tribune."

★ ★ ★

Talking to Your Vegetables

To another member of the Washington planning committee, the Prince of Wales explained his success as a gentleman gardener. He said that "to get the best results, you must talk to your vegetables." That theme was seconded at the party for her cabinet that Prime Minister Thatcher later gave at a London restaurant. The waiter deferentially approached the Prime Minjster, asking: "What will it be for you, Ma'am?" Mrs. Thatcher replied: "I'll have steak." The waiter continued: "And what about the vegetables?" "They'll have steak too," the Prime Minister replied.

Years later, at a Washington reception for retiring Secretary of State George Schultz, the Hugheses found themselves in a receiving line that included former Prime Minister Thatcher. TLH reintroduced himself to her, noting that they had first met in London thirty years earlier when she was the shadow Minister of Education and he was DCM for Ambassador Annenberg. She immediately brightened and said: "Well, they don't make them like that any more, do they!"

V

BACK HOME IN AMERICA
★ ★ ★

Nixon's Enemies List

After the defeat of the Labour Government in 1970, the Hugheses returned to Washington. TLH soon resigned from the government to accept the presidency of the Carnegie Endowment. In his rehabilitation years, after resigning from the Presidency, Nixon persisted in angling for an appearance at Carnegie. His bête noire, Alger Hiss, had once been president of Carnegie, and Nixon was obsessed with the idea of speaking on the premises. A dinner featuring a gratified Nixon was finally arranged. It was a matter of mutual convenience. Nixon's new role as elder statesman on foreign policy would be enhanced, as would Carnegie's reputation for non-partisanship.

The reporter Dan Schorr was in the audience. He had once been on Nixon's "enemies list." After dinner he went up to Nixon and said: "You probably don't remember me, Mr. President. I'm Dan Schorr." "Hell I don't!" Nixon replied. "Damn near hired you once!" That was the cover story for the telephone taps that Nixon had ordered years before— wiretapping his enemies as prospective appointees. Most officials can't remember their cover stories at all. With Nixon it was automatic recall.

Too Clever by Half

The Hugheses first crossed paths with the Helmut ("Hal") Sonnenfeldts in Washington in 1956 when Marjorie Sonnenfeldt and Jean Hughes worked together at the Democratic National Committee. (Jean was noticeably pregnant at the time, and when Adlai Stevenson visited the DNC, he asked her if she was going to last though the campaign. She did. Evan Hughes was born a month after Eisenhower's reelection). The Sonnenfeldts and the Hugheses subsequently remained good family friends for half a century.

In the 1950s Hal had been victimized by Otto Otepka, in one of Otepka's vendettas from the Office of Security at the State Department. Hal had taken refuge in the Arms Control and Disarmament Agency. In 1961, despite lingering objections in the State Department, Roger Hilsman and TLH rehabilitated Sonnenfeldt, bringing him back for a stellar career at INR. By the end of the Kennedy-Johnson years, Hal was generally acknowledged to be a leading, if not the leading, Sovietologist in town.

But Hal was also more than adept politically. In 1969 he effortlessly joined the Nixon administration when his old acquaintance, Henry Kissinger, asked him to serve in the White House. There he soon became known as "Kissinger's Kissinger," reflecting the somewhat nervous proximity of their relationship. In his memoirs Kissinger quotes an aide as saying: "Hal has the best intelligence system in town. Unfortunately it's aimed at you." The suspicions of Nixon and Kissinger about several of their subordinates were insatiable, and before long Sonnenfeldt found that his home telephone was one of those being tapped by Higher Authority.

It happened that, around that time, Hal occasionally stayed in TLH's Carnegie apartment when he was in New York. Once, while there, he apparently stumbled upon a list of contemporary Carnegie trustees. Aware that his phone was being tapped, Hal cleverly decided to turn the tables, converting a device set up for his own surveillance into an instrument that would ingratiate him with the White House perpetrators.

Suddenly TLH found himself on the receiving end of a puzzling phone call from Sonnenfeldt, who, in a matter-of-fact manner, said that he had been looking over the names of current Carnegie trustees. It seemed to him that there were very few, if any, friends of President Nixon on the Carnegie board. Hal then suggested the names of some good Nixonites (including Bebe Rebozo) who might be added to the Carnegie masthead, thereby enhancing the Endowment's reputation at the White House. TLH thanked Hal for his unsolicited advice, but was perplexed at the formality of the call from his old associate and friend. Perhaps he should have been pleased at the implied compliment that he was devious enough to have known what was going on.

A few days later another White House official informed TLH that the transcript of the Sonnenfeldt-Hughes phone call had promptly reached the Oval Office as Hal had intended, and that both Nixon and Kissinger had been deeply impressed by this genuine demonstration of Hal's loyalty.

"Give Peace a Chance"

At about the same time that Sonnenfeldt was urging TLH to Nixonize his board, the New York City premises of the Carnegie Endowment for International Peace had some other visitors that caused a big commotion out in the street. John and Yoko Lennon, whom Nixon considered a threat to US national security, came to give TLH a copy of their 1970s' antiwar anthem, "Give Peace a Chance." They also wanted to enlist TLH in John's visa problems with the FBI and INS who were trying to "neutralize" Lennon by deporting him as an undesirable alien. Deportation proceedings had already begun.

Their visit turned to disappointment, when TLH made it clear that Carnegie was a non-partisan institution. John and Yoko had mentioned that they were planning an anti-Nixon, get-out-the-vote, tour that would culminate at the 1972 Republican convention. Even autographing their pictures for the Hughes sons failed to produce real help. It seems there was nothing practical that Carnegie could do about John's visa.

John and Yoko must have written the Endowment off as a hopeless tool of the establishment. The Lennon lawsuits were dragged out by appeals and countersuits until 1975, when a federal judge finally overruled the INS. When Nixon was forced to resign over Watergate a year earlier, John Lennon's summary of the situation was: "I believe time wounds all heels."

A Success for the Swiss Embassy

In 1972 Nixon was reelected. In Puerto Rico, however, his friend, Governor Luis Ferre, was defeated by TLH's friend, Rafael Hernandez Colon. So the relationship between the White House and La Forteleza, the governor's mansion in San Juan, was expected to be frosty. The US Navy's continued use of the island of Culebra as a bombing range was a cause célèbre at the time,

Knowing that TLH's friend Elliot Richardson was then Nixon's Secretary of Defense, Hernandez-Colon suggested that TLH, as President of the Carnegie Endowment, take on a "Swiss Embassy role" and serve as an intermediary beneath the White House radar. TLH agreed to serve.

The first move from the Swiss Embassy was a petition against the naval bombardment. It was signed by Hernandez-Colon and all the previous governors of Puerto Rico, except Luis Ferre, Nixon's friend. TLH took the petition to Richardson in the Pentagon, where Elliot quickly noted the missing signature. "I'll make a deal", Richardson suggested. "If you get Ferre to sign your petition, I will stop the bombing." He probably counted on Ferre holding out for the navy's position.

The next weekend, ex-governor Ferre fortuitously took his yawl over to Culebra and anchored it off Dewey, Culebra's capital, appropriately named for the Spanish-American war admiral. The ex-governor started to take his siesta on board his boat, while the navy decided that this was the moment to open fire. Ferre's nap was abruptly interrupted by explosives zooming overhead, and by nightfall the anti-bombardment petition had the required new signature.

"Well, that was quick work," said Richardson rather ruefully, as he looked at Ferre's name and the now unanimous petition a few days later. "Over to you, Elliot," said the Swiss embassy. After several awkward reminders of his side of the bargain, Richardson's last act as Secretary of Defense, before becoming Attorney General, was to order the navy to stop bombing Culebra.

What Would Bismarck have Done?

On December 13, 1973, TLH walked across the street from the Carnegie Endowment in Washington to deliver a speech at the Woman's National Democratic Club. At the time his text was regarded as sensational, and copies were widely distributed to the press. The Watergate crisis was imminent, and the question of the hour was how long Kissinger would remain tied to Nixon's fate.

Brief quotes are suggestive of the line TLH took. Pointing to the similarities of Kissinger and Bismarck, he quoted A.G.P. Taylor's description of Bismarck: "He stood outside party or class, a solitary figure following a line of his own devising. He had no colleagues, only subordinates." Even Kissinger's jokes were reminiscent of Bismarck. The latter had once said maliciously to the liberal German Crown Prince: "I have sworn to observe the Constitution conscientiously, but what if my conscience tells me not to observe it?" Kissinger's up-dated version was: "The illegal we do immediately; the unconstitutional takes a little longer."

After comparing the respective predicaments of Bismarck and the Kaiser in 1890 with Nixon and Kissinger in 1973,

TLH suggested that "dropping the pilot" in 1973 argued for a reversal of roles, i.e. that in the national interest Kissinger should now help to drop Nixon.

An article in Time Magazine covered the speech extensively. Then to everyone's astonishment, the weekend editions of both the Washington Post and the New York Times published the full text simultaneously the following Sunday. It was the only such coincidence in the history of the rival newspapers.

Mao Confides in Kissinger

For some time Henry Kissinger turned the TLH article into a prolonged public joke. At Hal Sonnenfeldt's 1974 swearing in as counselor at the State Department, Kissinger announced from the podium: "And now, if you'll forgive me, I must greet an old friend who has been aiming shots across the bow. I see that my successor, Tom Hughes, has just entered the room. I will refrain, however, from kissing him on both cheeks, which is what I do now, ever since I was in Cairo, every time I see a man." Making his way across the room through a sea of admirals, generals, and spooks, and finally reaching TLH, he continued: " I told Mao that you would be much harder to deal with."

At a Kennedy Center reception following the opening of a Berlin Opera series in Washington, TLH went down the receiving line of visiting German dignitaries. Somehow Kissinger was also in the line-up, and he welcomed TLH with: "Ah, my successor!" The mayor of Berlin looked at both Hughes and Kissinger, wondering whether he had been given a cue to laugh. Henry then said solemnly: "That's what Chairman Mao told me. Tom Hughes is to be my successor." TLH added: "What a tribute to Chinese intelligence!"

Equally Famous Views

About that time, in a plane flying west from National Airport, TLH heard the pilot say: "Directly ahead of us on our line of ascent at about 11:00 o'clock, passengers on the left side of the aircraft can view the famous Watergate complex, while those on the right at about 1:00 o'clock, will have superb view of the equally famous Lincoln Memorial."

Attending a Bar Mitzvah

While he was Secretary of State, Kissinger was invited by the Israeli ambassador to attend the bar mitzvah of the ambassador's son. Henry accepted. At the conclusion of the ceremony, the ambassador came up to him and said: "Well, Mr. Secretary, this must have taken you back a good many years— perhaps to your own bar mitzvah." "No, no," Henry replied. "You see, Ribbentrop did not come to my bar mitzvah."

Ford's Slow Motion on China

In a 1974 article in the Atlantic on "Who Lost our China Policy?" TLH complained about the Ford administration's failure to finalize diplomatic relations with China and "put the finishing touches on the most farsighted, and widely praised, of Nixon's foreign policies." "Instead, Sino-American relations have come on more like George Bernard Shaw's description of Lady Halle's performance as pianist in the Beethoven septet. She took the first movement at about 2/3rds of the lowest speed needed to sustain life. The others followed her from note to note and thought of other things."

Kissinger Out of Office

In February, 1976, the last year of the Ford administration, TLH spoke at the Foreign Service Institute on "A World Without Kissinger and Other Impossibilities." He began: "It is now apparent that the greatest show on earth is gradually coming to a close. For years our foreign policy circus—the Ringling Brothers of Realpolitik, starring Henry Kissinger as the greatest lion tamer of them all—has drawn unrivalled acclaim."

"Years ago Kissinger himself cautioned: 'World politics is not a conjurer's business.' Yet in his heyday, Golda Meir was wont to say: 'Let us see what the magician brings.' Even now he remains the most celebrated of human cannon balls. Every time he volunteers to be stuffed once more into the cannon for shooting, onlookers exclaim: Where will we ever find someone of this caliber again?"

Despite the fact that political satire was said to have become impossible when Henry Kissinger got the Nobel Peace Prize, Henry continued to bask in the limelight. At a conference in Princeton he was discovered by a journalist, who excitedly came up to him waving her microphone and pleading "Dr. Kissinger, won't you please say something historic?" To which Henry relied: "Not to such a small group."

But later that day, in a press backgrounder, he asked: "And now, do you have a question for my answers?"

★ ★ ★

An Encounter in Bonn.

In the early 1990s TLH attended a lavish birthday party in Bonn for Walter Leisler Kiep, a German official who was being decorated by Queen Elizabeth. No sooner had the British consul risen to present the order to the German honoree, than the waiter dropped a huge tray, laden with the dinner plates that held the main course. There was a loud crash, and Kissinger, sitting across from TLH at the head table, said: "Another disaster for Anglo-German relations."

Making small talk in the interval while the kitchen recuperated, TLH told Henry that his new book "Diplomacy" was on full display, covering all the windows of a book store near Harvard Yard. In Cambridge for the day, TLH had been looking at this exhibit when two young Harvard students came up. The book's covers portrayed the famous scene of Bismarck at the 1878 Congress of Berlin with Disraeli and others in attendance. "And where is Dr. Kissinger in this picture?" the young woman was asking her boyfriend. TLH pointed immediately to Bismarck, and she said: "I think he's put on weight." TLH said he was doing what he could for Kissinger's reputation, and Henry said "Tom, you are very considerate."

★ ★ ★

The Best Man

In the 1980s Dimitri Simes, later head of the Nixon Center in Washington, was a senior associate at the Carnegie Endowment. He traveled to Russia with ex-President Nixon, and became a close advisor. One day people who had received invitations to Dmitri's wedding were told to be sure to be prompt in showing up at Dmitri's house, because the rabbi had a full schedule and couldn't be kept waiting. Therefore, on the appointed day, the guests were all milling around the garden in good time.

Suddenly there was a commotion from the street, including blaring police sirens. Minutes later a familiar figure burst through Dmitri's French doors leading to the garden. Nixon was flashing his victory sign. He was to be Dmitri's best man. The assembled crowd included a good many Democrats and long time Nixon-loathers. The wife of Carnegie's then president, Sheppie Abramowitz, said to Jean Hughes: "How the hell are we going to escape without shaking hands with him?" Jean said: "You're not. He will place himself right there at the door, and you had better think of something to say."

Sure enough, Nixon planted himself firmly astride the exit line. In a louder than conversational voice, he told TLH that the Carnegie Endowment had never been in better hands. TLH smiled uncomfortably, and told him how pleased we were to have Dmitri as a colleague. Jean told him that his last year's Christmas card—a family picture showing Nixon playing the piano—was "very effective." Sheppie mumbled something inoffensive. Miss Manners would have been proud of everyone.

★ ★ ★

Learn to Play the Piano

Nixon was, in fact, proud of his piano playing. In 1968 after his election he told the press: "For the first time in twenty years we're going to have a piano player in the White House. I play the piano, for example, Christmas carols. I can play all of the old timers, but I've got to learn the new tunes, the swingers."

It would be another tie that binds, shared on the other side of the world with his future friend, Chairman Mao Tse-tung. Mao addressed the subject in his little red book, available in 790 million copies. His essay, entitled "Learn to Play the Piano," can be found on pages 110-11. Mao advises: "In playing the piano, all ten fingers are in motion. It won't do to move some fingers only and not others. But if all ten fingers press down at once, there is no melody. To produce good music, the ten fingers should move in coordination. Wherever there is a problem, we must put our finger on it. This is a method we must master. Some play the piano well and some badly, and there is a great difference in the melodies they produce. We must all learn to play the piano well."

A Loser Gets Lost

In early 1973, after his 1972 defeat by Nixon, George McGovern dined with a group of guests at Gil and Nancy Harrison's. TLH and Jean were among them. During dinner McGovern excused himself and disappeared apparently in search of the men's room. After fifteen minutes, Nancy wondered aloud what had happened and went searching.

Eventually she found McGovern in their dark basement groping around, trying to find the lights or the stairs. Meanwhile at the dinner table, someone had suggested: "You don't suppose Tricky Dick has plumbers in the basement in this building too?

★ ★ ★

The British Embassy Marks the Bi-Centennial

In 1976 Queen Elizabeth and Prince Phillip came to Washington for the 200th anniversary of the Declaration of Independence. At the British Embassy garden party, the guests including TLH and his wife were hoping for a word or a glimpse. Ambassador Ramsbotham, resplendent with decorations and a sword at his side, promised to "bring Her Majesty around for a handshaking."

Meanwhile the Duke of Edinburgh was ambling around on his own, and suddenly he came up for some small talk. "Who's going to be picked as the Democratic candidate for Vice President?" he asked. TLH volunteered that Senator Walter Mondale would be Carter's best choice if he wanted to add strength to his ticket. In a surprising intervention in American politics, Phillip volunteered, in an off-handed manner, "I'm betting on him too." His bet turned out to be right.

★ ★ ★

The 1976 Vice Presidential Debate

Mondale called a group of friendly advisers including TLH to his Senate office, just before his Vice Presidential debate with Senator Dole in the 1976 campaign. As the briefing was about to wind down, Mondale asked "Does anyone have any final suggestions?" TLH said "Well, Dole is quite capable of bringing up 'Democrat wars.' It's one of his favorite themes. You should be ready to jump on it, if he happens to use it." In the event, just as predicted, Dole in fact did use the familiar phrase and Mondale was ready with a strong response.

After the election, Fritz recounted this episode on national television, giving "Tam Hughes" the credit for anticipating Dole's remark. "It won the debate, no doubt about it, and perhaps the election." Mondale recounted the episode twice more—in his memoirs, and in the 1996 Theodore Bogosian film, "Running Mate."

Bob Dole's Battle Plan

Many years later TLH received a four page letter "signed" by Bob Dole. It read: "I want you to know exactly how I can become President of the United States. That's why I've had this 1988 Dole-for-President Campaign Battle plan prepared especially for you. This document outlines my campaign strategy for 16 key states. Since it contains highly sensitive political information, your Battle Plan has been assigned serial number 00-952-774 and is registered with your name in my campaign headquarters."

To Be or Not to Be

In the fall of 1975, TLH published an article on "Populism and Foreign Policy." It prompted a letter from Plains,

Georgia, from Jimmy Carter who was then preparing to run for President. He wrote rather teasingly: "Your article is one of the most interesting I've ever read. It helped me toward deciding whether I'm a liberal or a populist. Thank you. Jimmy Carter."

Ted Sorensen Plans His Return

In the summer of 1976, during the Carter-Ford Presidential campaign, Ted Sorensen invited Zbig Brzezinski and TLH to have dinner with him at his New York apartment. He "thought it would be useful all around" for the three of them to discuss their respective aspirations for joining the prospective Carter Administration. "Let's sort things out, so that we won't get in one another's way," as Ted thoughtfully put it.

Zbig quickly announced that he intended to be National Security Adviser in a future Carter White House. He had already prepared the way by working closely with Jimmy in Trilateral Commission circles. Both Zbig and TLH had in fact recently addressed a Trilateral conference in Kyoto, Japan, with Carter in attendance.

To the surprise of the others, TLH said he did not intend to join a Carter administration. The presidency of the Carnegie Endowment was too good a job to give up, and he was going to remain there. Sorensen looked pleased and said "Well, that opens up several possibilities, including CIA."

The CIA: Twice Offered and Twice Declined

Shortly after Carter's election, Vice President-elect Mondale asked TLH to come to see him. Carter had told Mondale to supervise the recruitment of the new CIA director. Fritz had been active on Capital Hill in the recent investigations of the CIA by the Church committee, and he was sure that a massive cleanup at CIA was necessary. "After your eight years in INR, you are obviously the right guy to tackle this," Fritz said. But TLH declined. Apart from the prospect that, if he accepted, his wife might divorce him, he really didn't want to tackle the cleanup. Mondale pressed, but TLH remained firm.

Mondale and Carter then offered the CIA directorship to Ted Sorensen who quickly agreed. Before long he ran into a buzz-saw of opposition on Capitol Hill. Ted had been a conscientious objector in World War II, and that didn't help. Nor did allegations that he had taken classified material away with him when he left the White House to write his book about Kennedy. Soon the Sorensen confirmation was in deep trouble, and Carter offered him little or no support.

Shortly before the inauguration, the Minnesota State Society gave a testimonial dinner at a Washington hotel for Minnesota's two Vice Presidents– Humphrey and Mondale. When the Marine Guard started playing the Star Spangled Banner, TLH found himself standing between the two of them. When the music stopped, Fritz turned to Hubert and said: "We're running into trouble on the CIA director. Sorensen isn't confirmable. Tell Tom he has to take it. Everyone has recommended him–Rusk, Vance, Harriman, Linowitz, Colby, Helms, everybody."

Humphrey said: "Tom, you really have to take it." TLH said, "Sorry, old friend, but I don't and I can't. By the way, however, there's a Rhodes Scholar classmate of Carter's at Annapolis whom you might take a look at—Admiral Stansfield Turner." One thing led to another, and Turner got the job.

Watching the Panama Vote in Havana

Hearing that TLH was to visit Cuba unofficially during the Carter administration, Brzezinski asked him to deliver a message to Castro warning him that Cuba's expeditionary adventures in the Ogaden were not worth the risk of World War III. While waiting to see Fidel, TLH was entertained by his deputy, Carlos Rafael Rodriguiz. It was the night of the Senate vote in Washington on the Panama Canal treaty, and earlier that day Rodriguiz had given Castro his Senator-by-Senator predictions. Suddenly, De Concini voted the wrong way. "Damn DeConcini. He's unpredictable! Fidel will never let me forget this one."

With Best Personal Regards

After the "malaise" crisis in the Carter administration, Hedley Donovan was brought into the White House as a high level advisor. People who had known Hedley as the editor of Time, or as a Carnegie Endowment trustee, were aware of his taciturn qualities. It was never very clear what he was supposed to do in Washington, or what he was actually doing. In 1980

Hedley thanked the President for the enjoyable months he had spent in the White House, but added that, in fairness, Carter should know that he would be unable to vote for him for re-election. Privately, Hedley had concluded that being born again was no substitute for growing up.

★ ★ ★

The Chairmen Visit

On state occasions TLH and Jean were on the guest list of the Soviet Embassy in Washington. The ambassadors themselves ranged from the ineffective "Smiling Mike" Menshikov to the astute and long-serving Anatoli Dobrynin.

The embassy's most memorable official visitors were Nikita Khrushchev in September, 1959, and Mikhail Gorbachev in December, 1987. At the embassy lunch for Gorbachev, TLH found himself sitting between Senator Eugene McCarthy and Douglas Fairbanks Jr., whom Gorbachev implausibly described as his "old friends." Détente dominated the agenda, and TLH politely refrained from asking Fairbanks for the truth about his alleged encounter with the Duchess of Argyll (see "Other Photos of Interest" above.)

★ ★ ★

Extra-Curricular Connections

After leaving government service, TLH kept involved in current affairs, not only professionally at the Carnegie Endowment, but also through links to academia. His advisory board affiliations included the Center for International Studies (Harvard,) the Woodrow Wilson School (Princeton,) the

School of Foreign Service (Georgetown,) the Humphrey Institute of Public Affairs (Minnesota), the Korbel Institute (Denver), the Fundacion Luis Munoz Marin (Puerto Rico), and the Ditchley Foundation (England).

TLH's NGO trusteeships included the Arms Control Association, the Atlantic Council, the International Institute of Strategic Studies, and the American Institute of Contemporary German Studies. He was a founding trustee of the German Marshall Fund of the US, and secretary-treasurer of the American Academy of Berlin. He served as president of the Washington Institute of Foreign Affairs, chairman of the editorial board of Foreign Policy Magazine, and chairman of the Mid-Atlantic Club of Washington. In retirement he has been a Distinguished Visiting Research Scholar at the German Historical Institute (Washington).

VI

DIPLOMATS, SOLDIERS, AND BUREAUCRATS

★ ★ ★

American Diplomatic Virtues

In the 1970s someone had the foresight to request the Foreign Service Selection Board to preserve memorable comments from a review they had just made of Foreign Service professionals. Each one of these was actually written by a rating officer about one of his FSO colleagues:

"He made no blunder or mistakes in the period under review, a remarkable record.

"His unflappability is impeccable.

"He is well above average, even among Foreign Service Officers.

"Although just starting married life, he is well on his way to acquiring an interesting collection of books.

" His conduct is exemplary, which means he enjoys life, while keeping in mind that he is a Foreign Service Officer.

"He is an extrovert in manner, an introvert in thought.

"He is humanly weaker in some respects than others, but his faults are not obtrusive.

"He gives lucid analyses of incomprehensible subjects, e. g. "As Jesus Christ once said, and rightly so…"

"I have awarded him the highest mark possible—satisfactory with distinction.

"He has a tendency toward excessive colloquy, but he is overcoming his enchantment with the passive voice.

"The Angel Gabriel could not have improved on his performance."

Advice to Speakers

A directive from the Foreign Service Institute in the 1960s was designed to help senior speakers address the "Basic Officers Course." "We must establish rapport with our junior officers. We have found that the communication of ideas and concepts, particularly between individuals of different generations, can be difficult and require more skill than is usually assumed… We recommend that a speaker enliven his presentation by recalling personal experiences, while nevertheless avoiding excessive use of low level anecdotes."

Red Teams and Blue

In the 1960s the reds were still leftists and the blues were still rightists, as they had been, historically, around the world. War games were in vogue at the Pentagon, and the deepening morass in Vietnam was often the subject of war gaming. John McNaughton, a key McNamara adviser, asked TLH to take part in one of them. He assigned TLH a role with the Viet Cong. In the intellectual give and take that followed, McNaughton complimented TLH on "behaving like a true member of the red team"—not exactly a term of endearment for the ears of the uniformed, arm-chaired, anti-communists who filled the room.

Of course in today's America, red means Republican and blue means Democratic. How this curious reversal of colors came about is unknown and its historical oddity is not even wondered at. Probably it was popularized by some media innocent, and obediently adopted by a national audience, totally undisturbed by perpetrating this violence on a tradition that had been well-established for centuries.

Quick Trips

In the 1960s when Angier Biddle Duke was named ambassador, his was said to be "the fastest trip in history from the El Morocco to El Salvador."

His colleague, Bill Roundtree, was appointed ambassador to Brazil shortly after Brasilia was chosen as the new capital. Brasilia was primitive territory in those days, and Mrs. Roundtree flew up from Rio to inspect it. Just as she anticipated, she found Brasilia unsatisfactory, and she quickly flew back to Rio. Thereafter she was familiarly known as "Mrs. Roundtrip."

Venice as a Hardship Post

Bill Crawford served in the American Consulate in Venice in its final days. He said that they had little to do, apart from serving Peggy Guggenheim. Every year or so she would come in and announce: "It's happened again! My passport fell into the canal." The staff began to notice that every time Peggy filled out her application for passport renewal, her birth date was later, by two or three years. Staff meetings discussed whether the consulate should continue with this illegal charade, but they regularly decided that no one but Peggy would go to jail if it ever became an issue. So Peggy became younger and younger as the years went on. The consulate itself, however, died of old age and was finally closed for lack of business.

Shots in Stockholm

On September 11, 1973, TLH found himself in Stockholm, for a scheduled interview with Alva Myrdal at the Swedish Foreign Ministry. On arrival he noticed that the loud speaker system seemed to be broadcasting events from Chile throughout the building. As he sat down opposite Mrs. Myrdal, shots rang out in the background and she said: "I'm afraid, Mr. Hughes, that you have just assassinated President Allende of Chile." Without pursuing matters, TLH suggested that perhaps another time would be more propitious for the interview, and he quietly said goodbye.

Spousal Consequences

Douglas MacArthur II, the famous general's nephew, served in Japan from 1957-61 as ambassador. He was married to the indomitable Wahwee Barkley, the daughter of Vice President Alben Barkley. On one important ceremonial occasion the MacArthurs joined Japanese Prime Minister Kishi and his wife on their first postwar visit to an important but controversial shrine, located some distance from Tokyo.

Having grown up in Kentucky, Wahwee had a lifelong familiarity with Jack Daniels whiskey. She normally carried a flask of it on her appointed rounds. On this occasion, she was seated with the prime minister's wife in the back seat of official car # 2. Car #1, with the ambassador and the prime minister, preceded them with bumper flags flying.

Facing a thirty mile trip, Wahwee reached for her flask on departing Tokyo, and took a snort of Jack Daniels. She then hospitably offered a swig to her companion. For Mrs. Kishi, bourbon was a totally new experience. She took an immediate liking to it, and as the procession proceeded, Wahwee's flask went back and forth in the rear of car #2.

Arriving at the shrine, car #1 came to its scheduled halt. The Japanese Defense Forces band started playing the national anthems, and TV covered the arrival ceremonies for a nation-wide audience. The ambassador and prime minister emerged smartly from car #1. Car # 2 then arrived at the appointed place. The rear left door opened, and Wahwee emerged, no worse for wear. But when the right rear door opened, Mrs. Kishi tumbled out unsteadily and quickly rolled down an adjacent ravine. The band music ceased, but the TV cameras pursued the Japanese defense forces, as they rushed down the hillside to rescue the latest unintended victim of American diplomatic outreach.

★ ★ ★

Our Ally in Peshawar

As part of its military aid program, the US since the 1950s had provided its "ally" Pakistan with extensive intercept equipment to be targeted on the Soviet Union. When Director of INR, TLH visited Peshawar in 1964 and was given a ceremonial bagpipe welcome, including a parade by Pak soldiers dressed in Scottish kilts. He was proudly shown the intelligence gathering center where the American-provided antennae were pointed directly north toward their Soviet targets.

After a gala luncheon, TLH returned to his official car to leave. When driving past the intercept station again, he could not help but notice that the antennae were now pointing directly east. When he mentioned this to the driver, he was told: "Oh, Sir, they've returned now to their normal position," i.e., aimed at India.

On leaving Pakistan, TLH remembered Lord Carrington's praise for the astuteness of foreign governments that sent their young men to Sandhurst instead of to the London School of

Economics. "A Sandhurst education is more useful than that of LSE, when the coup comes."

The Extended Nehru Family

On TLH's first trip to India in 1964, Chet Bowles, ambassador there again, had suggested that TLH should by all means see Madam Pandit, Nehru's charming but formidable sister. She had been ambassador to the UN and was well known in America. In due course, TLH was invited to dinner with "Nan" in what was then called Bombay. After a pleasant discussion, TLH made the mistake of asking whether she often visited Delhi these days. "Delhi, no, not really. That's my niece's territory."

In due course, her niece, Indira Gandhi, became Prime Minister. Official relations with the US were strained under Nixon and Kissinger. They had warmed to Pakistan and had used it as a springboard for their opening to China. Indira was also suspicious of American behavior inside India, from the CIA to the Ford Foundation. In Washington TLH was president at Carnegie, and Indian Ambassador K. R. Narayanan, who later became President of India, thought that the US non-governmental community might pick up some of the slack in the Indo-American relationship. Since TLH was going to visit India, Narayanan insisted on setting up a visit with the Prime Minister so that TLH could enlighten her about American NGOs.

In Delhi the appointed day arrived and TLH presented himself at Mrs. Gandhi's parliamentary office, adjoining the Lok Sahba. He was shown into an empty room and told to wait. A note taker soon arrived, and then the lady herself. After a rather stiff handshake, it was clear that she was in one of her moods. She began to stare out of the window. TLH concluded that it was up to him to warm things up, so he started to improvise on the role of NGOs in America. He mentioned that Ambassador Narayanan thought that perhaps NGOs could be useful at a time when government-to-government relations were in something of a slump. Pause. There was no response from the Prime Minister.

TLH resumed extemporizing on the wide variety of subjects that American NGOs were addressing these days. After two or three minutes he paused again. There was still no response from Mrs. Gandhi. TLH steeled himself for a third and final attempt to stimulate conversation. Still unsuccessful, he lapsed into silence himself.

Indira Gandhi finally bestirred herself and said: "Oh, I suppose it is possible to get along, at some level, with countries with whom we have fundamental disagreements. For example, I am leaving for England tomorrow to open an Anglo-Indian conference in London. So we sometimes find it possible to have passable relations, even with the British. But with YOU!"

TLH figured that this signaled the end of his visit. So he thanked the Prime Minster for receiving him and took his leave. Bowles, Galbraith and others who knew Indira, claimed that when the spirit moved, she could be charming. She was a convinced socialist, like her brother. One wondered how she reacted when she learned that there was a "Nehru Center of Free Enterprise and Business" at Cambridge University!

★ ★ ★

Counting Elephants

A few years later TLH was leaving Delhi by taxi for the Indira Gandhi Airport, when the driver suddenly slowed. "Look over there, Sir." A procession of elephants was crossing the highway. "What do we do now?" "Ve vait." "What shall we do while we're waiting?" "We could try to name each elephant for an American ambassador to India," said the intelligent taxi driver. So we started and managed to think of eight—George Allen, Chester Bowles. John Sherman Cooper, Kenneth Keating, Bob Goheen, Ken Galbraith, Elsworth Bunker, and Harry Barnes. "But, sir, there are nine elephants." " We must count Chester Bowles twice."

After the Cultural Revolution

In 1975 some twenty American foundation executives spent three weeks in China. The group was headed by Cyrus Vance, not yet Secretary of State, who was then representing the Council on Foreign Relations. Arriving at Beijing airport, the visitors found a fleet of official cars waiting to escort them. John Knowles, then president of the Rockefeller Foundation, guessed that there would be contests among Vance and other "leaders" in the delegation to commandeer cars #1 and #2. TLH suggested that the two of them simply get into car #4 and avoid the struggle for preference.

It turned out that #4's driver spoke fair English. He welcomed his American passengers by saying, "You must be very important people. China is only receiving future world leaders this year." Asked who had visited recently, he replied

"Dr. Franz Josef Strauss" who, the Chinese apparently assumed, was going to be the next West German Chancellor. Strauss had given the driver a Bavarian hunting rifle, which the driver was hoping to keep. The authorities were telling him to surrender the rifle as a gift from a state visitor. With the issue still unresolved, the driver of car #4 hoped that Knowles and Hughes would intercede on his behalf with the decision-makers.

Spittoons Still in Service

In 1975 in Beijing's Great Hall of the People, the twenty Americans settled in for an interview with Deng Xiaoping. Deng was sitting in an armchair in the center of a pale beige carpet that stretched across the room. Several polished brass spittoons were strategically placed fifteen to twenty feet from Deng. The interview inself was punctuated with sudden eruptions and gushers from Deng, whose liquid missives were variously, but unerringly, directed toward the distant spittoons. The immaculate white carpet seemed to testify to the chairman's excellent aim during this, and many past, interviews.

Mrs. Luce's Delayed Response to TLH

Clare Booth Luce, femme fatale, former ambassador to Italy, and member of PFIAB, phoned TLH from her house in Honolulu in November, 1977. "Is this that nice Mr. Hughes whose scintillating farewell lectures on intelligence I read after he left INR back in 1969? It is? Well it's Clare Booth Luce calling from Hawaii to beg forgiveness. He must have wondered why he never heard from me. Of course, he didn't hear from me, because I never mailed the long letter that I wrote him. Here it is, right here on my desk, un-mailed all these years. Can you believe it? So, finally, I am calling that nice Mr. Hughes to read my letter to him now, rather belatedly, over the phone."

Mrs. Luce's Delayed Disclosure to Bill Colby

A year earlier, Mrs. Luce successfully mailed a letter to Bill Colby, a friend of hers who had become CIA Director. She recalled Senator Keating's premature public allegations about a Soviet missile buildup in Cuba, that had so agitated the Kennedy administration in the weeks before their actual discovery in October, 1962. Despite repeated requests, Keating himself had always refused to disclose his source.

Clare now told Colby that she was the source. Conducting her own private foreign policy, she had personally hired boats for Cuban exiles in Florida to go back to the island and return with information. They were the ones who had seen the large crates, and Clare was the one who told Keating about them. She also urged her editor-husband to press for an invasion of Cuba, which Life Magazine promptly did, before the U-2 flights verified the actual missile deployment. Both Luces considered themselves to be conductors of foreign policy by remote control.

Mrs. Luce Exhausts a Secret Agent

About this time people also began learning of Roald Dahl's exploits as a seductive spy attached to the British Embassy in Washington in 1940-1. Like that of other covert agents, his objective was to encourage American entry into the war at the earliest possible date. A dashing young bon vivant and well-known author, he was officially ordered to become intimate with Clare Booth Luce. By all reports he was highly successful, and, as with Cuba later, Life Magazine, under her husband's editorship, was ahead of events in advocating a declaration of war.

After several weeks of patriotic service, however, Dahl complained to Ambassador Halifax that he was utterly exhausted by the Luce assignment. He asked to be relieved. The ambassador apparently told him: "You are under orders from London that I cannot countermand. Better just shut your eyes and think of England."

"And I am Marie of Rumania"

Among TLH's neighbors in Chevy Chase was the formidable Ambassador Joseph Green, a legendary State Department figure from the past. He had been responsible for Foreign Service recruitment in the 20s and 30s, when he had preferred Princetonians in general and George Kennan in particular.

One day Ambassador Green described his assignment to Rumania in the heyday of Queen Marie. Over tea at the palace in Bucharest, she had quizzed him about his family origins. After he described his ancestral connections with the

American Revolution and the American Civil War, the queen said, "How very interesting, Mr. Green. As for myself, my grandmother was Queen Victoria, and my grandfather was Czar Alexander II, and that's tip top socially around here."

The White House Phone

Now, in his old age and wearing a French beret, Ambassador Green became a companion of the young Hughes boys across the street. One day in the '60s he took them for a walk around the neighborhood. En route they told him about the special phone at their house that was equipped with a "may-I-help-you lady." They soon invited him up to their father's study to inspect it. Just as advertised, when he lifted the receiver, the White House operator said: "May I help you?"

Mid-Flight Angst

Once when on duty with Barry Goldwater's 9999th Air Force Reserve Squadron, the sleeping reservists were awakened at midnight over the mid-Atlantic by a voice from the cockpit: "Gentlemen, you might want to know that the commander, General Goldwater himself, is now at the controls." The news that the senator was actually piloting the plane was enough to cause most of the deepest sleepers to wake up.

To calm his nerves after this abrupt announcement, TLH took from his suitcase his wife's copy of Mary McCarthy's "The Group", a recently published expose of life at Vassar, where Jean had gone to college. After leaving the cockpit,

Goldwater sauntered back through the cabin. Stopping at TLH's seat, he leafed through the book. "Not worth reading" was his instant verdict. "That's what the trash bin is for!"

The Name Escapes Me

In Washington retirement circles, a story began to circulate. John Lord O'Brien, the nearly 90-year-old-dean of Washington lawyers, was back in Cambridge for his 70th Harvard reunion. He was reported to have wandered around Harvard Yard until he spied a face from the past that seemed vaguely familiar. He would then go up to its owner, stretch out his hand, and say: "My name is John Lord O'Brien. Can you remember yours?" And his fellow alumnus would reply: "Let me see, O'Brien, was it you or your brother who was killed in the Great War?"

The Name Escapes Me Again

In June, 1963, a French diplomat in Washington, Andre Visson, hosted a farewell dinner party for the George McGhees. George was about to take up his new post as ambassador to West Germany. Representative Jim Fulton from Pittsburgh was one of the guests, and at dinner's end, the congressman was moved to toast the diplomatic pair. But he couldn't remember Cele McGhee's first name, so he whispered urgently to his hostess: "What's her first name?" "Assia," said Madam Visson who thought she was being asked for her own.

The congressman then stood up and, after many laudatory remarks about Ambassador McGhee, said he knew that George and Assia would be a terribly successful team in Bonn. Cele McGhee quickly lept to her feet and said to her husband: "I hope that you and Assia will be very happy in Bonn and totally successful in your joint mission there. Andre and I will miss you so much."

Glimpses of the Harrimans

At the Harrimans' in Georgetown for a dinner sometime in the '70s, one of the guests asked Pamela whether it was really true that she had advised her then father-in-law, Winston Churchill, that June 5/6, 1944, would be the optimum date for the invasion of Normandy . "Oh yes," said Pamela cheerfully, "I knew that would be the right time for D-Day, because General Rommel would be away from Normandy then, celebrating his wedding anniversary back in Germany." The woman next to TLH whispered: "Isn't it remarkable that Pamela, at such an early age, had a Rolodex listing the wedding dates of German generals?"

In the 1980s the Carnegie Endowment installed its first office computers. TLH had dictated a letter to Pamela Harriman, and his secretary was typing it up on her new IBM Word Perfect. Suddenly the machine balked, and a message appeared on the screen: "The word Harriman is unknown to IBM Word Perfect. Try 'harridan'."

As Averell Harriman grew older, Pamela favored small dinners for him. One night it was old home week on Vietnam with the Ellsworth Bunkers and the Hugheses. Averell, known to intimates as "the crocodile," was just back from Barbados, more irascible than ever. And this time, in early 1984, he had a broken limb.

Harriman began to reminisce about his peace talks in Paris in 1968. "If it hadn't have been for the obstruction of that ambassador of ours out in Saigon, Humphrey would easily have won the election." "Now be careful, Averell," Pamela would say, "Ellsworth here was our ambassador in Saigon."

At a lunch at the Harriman estate in Middleburg, Virginia, in the 1970s, the guests were then German ambassador, Berndt von Staden, and his charming wife, Wendy von Neurath, niece of the one time German Foreign Minister. Averell suddenly proclaimed, apropos of nothing in particular, "the trouble with the Germans is that they have never known how to get along with the Soviet Union. I learned how, long ago."

Toward the end of Averell's life, Pamela phoned that she would be away that night, but would send a car to pick up Joe Kraft, the journalist, and TLH to be driven to Middleburg to keep Averell company for the evening. Once there, Averell started to describe a large bronze sculpture on his library table. He said it was the work of his brother- in- law, whose name he couldn't remember.

In an effort to retrieve the name, Averell thought that perhaps he had mentioned the sculptor in his memoirs, a book recently published, whose title he also could not recall. He naturally assumed that Kraft and Hughes would have read his memoirs and would know the title. So perhaps they could search the bookshelves for a copy. Unsuccessful at ground level, Joe Kraft climbed up a tall book ladder to the top shelf of the Harriman library to look for the Harriman memoirs. But that too proved a futile exercise and, after a vain search that lasted ten minutes or so, the butler mercifully announced dinner. It was the last time we saw the legendary "governor."

Early in the Clinton Administration, Pamela Harriman's ambassadorial confirmation hearings reached an impasse when Senator Jesse Helms attempted to impugn her patriotism by suggesting that she was secretly a supporter of European federalism. Stimulated by his staff research, Helms said he had discovered that Pamela actually belonged to the "Monnet Society." He asked her to confirm that she shared Monnet's 'federalist vision of an integrated Europe."

Somewhat flustered, Pamela replied: "Senator, I do not think I am involved in the Monnet Society." Rather baffled, she then spun around in confusion looking for help. After a whispered conversation with a quick- thinking advisor, she looked immensely relieved and exclaimed: "Oh, it is Claude Monet, the painter, the artist. I have made a contribution to restore his home." There were chuckles all around, except for the Senator from North Carolina and his staff, for whom both Jean Monnet and Claude Monet were totally new acquaintances.

More Fallout from Vietnam

Mrs. George Ball's name was Ruth. In the 1960s when George was dictating his memos opposing the Vietnam War, he occasionally got swept away. After mispronouncing the phrase "ruthless use of force" a few times, making it come out as "useless ruth," he finally said to his secretary, "For God's sake, don't tell Ruth!"

Revisionist Praise

In the 1980s a testimonial dinner, honoring George Ball, was organized by his business associates in New York. Speeches were made by a remarkable group of people, including several who had not hitherto been known for their devotion to George or his views when he was Undersecretary of State. They were now repeatedly professing the contrary. One outstandingly implausible witness disclosed something that he had "never confessed, even to my wife. George Ball was a model for me throughout my days in the White House."

At this point, several listeners looked down at their dinner plates in embarrassment. TLH sent a note to the speaker's former White House colleague, Karl Kaysen. "This sounds very much like what Justice Brandeis had in mind when he declared that Theodore Roosevelt had "the gift of contemporaneous sincerity," i.e. he was sincere at the time he said it. Kaysen wrote back: "Have you ever come across the Hebrew word Lehavdel? It means 'appropriate for the moment, but not to be remembered afterwards.' Apropos."

Hemispheric Affairs

Shortly before their marriage in 1995, Jane and TLH
were guests at a large reception at the Embassy of Peru in
Washington. TLH had almost forgotten the florid excesses
of Latin American culture. A bald and portly Peruvian
diplomat—apparently an old admirer of Jane's from her years
in Peru—approached from across the room, clasped TLH
with both hands, and said "I want to congratulate you on your
superb achievement." –meaning, apparently, capturing Jane
from a famously crowded field of suitors.

★ ★ ★

The Dean

The dean of the diplomatic corps in the 1960s was
Ambassador Sevilla Sacasa of Nicaragua. He was the senior
ambassador in length of service, probably because his wife
was a member of the long-lived Somoza dynasty. The
ambassador's standard uniform was white tie and tails,
which he had an opportunity to wear more or less daily.
Along with the tails, he sported a broad orange sash
which set him apart from his more ordinary diplomatic
colleagues.

TLH once found himself vis-a-vis Sevilla Sacasa in a
situation which called for some small talk. Trying to rise to
the occasion. TLH inquired whether the ambassador often
went on visits home. "Home? Home? Nicaragua? Why should
I? Not for at least fifteen years!" In response, TLH mumbled

that, of course, that was understandable, since he had so many taxing responsibilities here."

Dining Out In Havana

In 1999 TLH and Jane visited Cuba as part of a group of Latin Americanists from Johns Hopkins university. One evening in Havana, they all had dinner at a paladar, a private home licensed by the government to entertain paying guests. The host urged everyone to enjoy the surroundings, admire his paintings, look at his book collection, and savor the dinner. "I have only one request," he said. "When you leave, take me with you, please!"

Pope John Paul had recently visited Cuba, and according to the cardinal there had been a few days of relaxation from normal governmental restrictions. Things had tightened up again with the Pope's departure. "You realize," the cardinal said, "the brain drain from Cuba has resumed—mostly to Angola, where we once had an expeditionary force. When they returned from Africa, our soldiers told their wives about it, and many have decided to emigrate. As the saying goes, 'How are you going to keep them back in Havana, once they've seen Luanda?'"

Holbrooke Arranges Dinner

Richard Holbrooke and TLH were close associates at the Carnegie Endowment in the 1970s, when Dick was managing editor of Foreign Policy magazine. His famous entrepreneurial instincts were already in play. One day, without consulting the prospective hosts in advance, he announced that he had "arranged a small dinner to be held at your house next Thursday night. Ted Kennedy, Frank Church, Mrs. Church, and Blythe Babiak (then Dick's partner) are coming, and Blythe, of course, should be seated between the two senators."

Holbrooke Re-recollects

In May, 1998, Jane and TLH were in Berlin at Newsweek correspondent Andrew Nagorski's apartment where several other journalists were gathered. They had just been debriefing Richard Holbrooke, who was fresh from Belgrade and his last conversation with Slobodan Milosevic. Dick, of course, already had his sights set on becoming diplomat-of-the-century.

New York Times correspondent Roger Cohen asked Dick how he had left things with the Serbian leader and what his parting words had been. "I just said 'Hasta la Vista", said Holbrooke. "Oh, too bad. Why didn't you say something historic?" "Like what?" asked Dick. "You could have said: 'The future is entirely up to you, Slobodan'." A half hour later, the same journalists turned on Berlin TV only to find Holbrook facing the cameras. He was asked the same question about his final words in Belgrade. "Oh," Dick replied, "I simply said: 'The future is entirely up to you Slobodan'." Holbrooke's reply was now more historic, with a little help from his friends.

Adjusting Upwards in Washington

In the 1970s, Holbrooke was the managing editor of
Foreign Policy magazine, then the flagship publication of
the Carnegie Endowment. TLH was chairman of the board,
and he and other board members watched as Holbrooke's
meteoric career took off. As he kept ascending, however,
so did his Who's Who account. Before long it dropped
"managing" and Richard emerged as FP's full-fledged
"editor." Who could contradict him—except, perhaps,
the real editors, Warren Manshel and Sam Huntington.

Adjusting Downwards in London

Staff meetings in the American Embassy in London
in the 1970s were often similarly entertaining. People
waited for the politically correct readjustments of British
politicians as they annually updated, or downgraded,
their sketches in Who's Who to accord with their current
political needs.

Thus, as Anthony Wedgwood Benn strove leftwards
to lead the Labour Party's left wing, he kept adjusting
downward his biographic account. Lord Stansgate, his father,
was the first to be deleted, as presumably too embarrassing a
parent for the Labour-Left. The following year Winchester,
Tony's prep school, was deleted, probably as hopelessly elitist.
Tony-watchers would bet on what the next year's excisions
would be.

Will the Meeting Come to Order?

"I lived in the Government of the United States for many years," Woodrow Wilson once wrote, "and I never saw the Government of the United States." That government is particularly hard to find in the phenomenon of inter-agency meetings. Some of TLH's notes from inter-agency sessions remain vivid:

–of John McCone, the Director of CIA, who unfortunately, had been told by JFK that he would also be a policy maker. McCone, putting on his "policy hat" at interagency meetings, would then turn to one of his CIA deputies and inquire: "Does the CIA wish to speak?"

–of the ranking British visitor who told his American counterpart after a day of briefings in Washington on the Middle East: "Oh, I agree with you of course, but your people don't."

–of an admiral who freely confessed that the navy classified information merely to keep it out of the hands of Defense Department civilians.

The Bureaucratic Free-for-All

From an ambassador in a communist capital: "The President tells me that I am in charge of all official U.S. activities here. My military attaches seem not to have absorbed this fact. Can the Secretary of State please help me restrain excessive collection of unwanted information by my attaches?" (Tentative answer: no.)

From CIA: "The Secretary of Defense and I developed this plan. I charged my station chief to prepare an analysis pursuant thereto. If the generals can't use our product, screw them."

From NSA: "God knows we have other problems, but lack of office space is no excuse for failure anywhere in the world."

From State: "Why do we have to send this China estimate overseas, just because that's where the action is? That's where the leaking is too. There will be lots less mischief if we keep it here in Washington."

From CIA: "I will not sit here with responsibility for these expensive technological failures and have this go on. Maybe the Pentagon's got the wrong team operating this again. I'm dissatisfied, and so is the President, when I get through talking to him."

From the Air Force representative to his State Department colleague after the meeting breaks up: "I personally agree with every word in your dissenting footnote, but the Air Force thinks otherwise."

★ ★ ★

The Inter-Agency Round Table

From NSA: "I see the State Department doesn't want me to go to Africa or Latin America these days. Actually, our record was very good, except on the day it happened."

From State: "It's ridiculous not to be able to get damage assessments on civilian casualties, non-military targets hit, and military targets missed."

From the Pentagon: "that's not intelligence—that's operations."

From the Army: "Back to our old friend, cost-effectiveness—ignored as usual, for the usual good reasons."

From CIA: "The Director is statutorily charged with protection of intelligence sources and methods. Therefore he can override the National Security Council and take the matter directly to Capitol Hill. I doubt he will want to do so in this particular case."

From the FBI: "The Attorney General is showing an intense personal interest in national intelligence estimates and demanding the completion of this one at once. " Others: "If he wants it bad enough, he'll get it bad enough."

From State, as the fall session gets underway at the United Nations: "The annual unpleasantness is about to begin."

From the Army: "How did the White House expect us to predict what happened in Panama? Do they think we have the foresight to put Balboa High School students on the payroll?"

From NSA: "I'm sure we all have problems with the interpretation just given by the CIA representative. Let's let him continue to give the regulations his interpretation, and the rest of us will continue to read them as written."

From DIA: "Shouldn't we say something about the Cultural Revolution?" CIA: "We asked the Sinologists not to predict on this one. Their ignorance is so great that they would make us all look silly later."

Getting Down to Serious Subjects

From the Army: "Is it only in Africa that people are refusing to cooperate in the American national interest?" Chorus: "No, everywhere." CIA: "Their cooperation has to be bought like any business transaction." Army: "Apparently they are not for sale."

From General X: "Outer space is free, just as free as the high seas. Free Seas, Free Space." Admiral Y:" That may help with satellites, but it doesn't help make U-2s lawful. They fly in the atmosphere, not in space." General Z: "But we're flying U-2s over countries that we don't recognize. So they're legal too."

From Defense: "Let's delete the sentence 'The day of colonialism in Africa is drawing to a close.'" From State: "Let's retain the sentence, inserting 'has drawn'." From CIA: "Let's remove these Political Science 101 statements. I am sure our policy makers have these maxims well in mind." From State: "We should not be too sure how many of these maxims our policy makers have in mind."

From NSA: "I confess I'm not at all sure what this means, but I find it very hard to oppose…Do we ever consider the cost to the reader of taking up his time on irrelevant matters?"

From FBI: "All of us would be better off sticking to certitudes and not speculating about communist intentions." CIA: "Estimating begins when certitude ends." FBI: "I disagree." (Around the table: smothered laughter).

The Chairman: "Let's take the marijuana out of this exercise."

Admiral Crowe Recalls

In 2002 when Admiral William Crowe was chairman, and TLH was president, of the Washington Institute of Foreign Affairs, Crowe enjoyed telling about two celebrated after dinner speeches he remembered. One was of a farewell party for a general who was accustomed to reading the speeches prepared for him by his subordinates. He rose at his own testimonial dinner, and finding the text of the guest speaker's speech already on the podium, he began reading a speech in praise of himself.

At a similar dinner in honor of Admiral Jerauld Wright, there was an invited guest speaker. But Wright took the podium ahead of him and proceeded to reminisce about his life in the navy. He launched on a reprise of his entire career beginning, "Now, on my first ship…" He was still on his first ship some fifteen minutes later, and the audience was murmuring, "How many ships did he have?" The chairman finally rose to save the situation, saying "That is wonderful, Admiral, and we all look forward to hearing about the other ships you commanded. Meanwhile, I am going to introduce our guest speaker who has a few things to say about your record of service on board those very ships, and so I present..."

A Thirst for Travel

When the State Department first expressed its doubts about the propriety of personal visits between CIA Director McCone and foreign heads of state, the Director replied: "The President wants me personally to go to visit heads of state to brief them on matters which are too sensitive for their foreign ministers. The fact that I took the trouble to come personally made a deep impression on Chancellor Erhard.

"American ambassadors always welcome my visits— nothing personal, just a tribute to the advantage of dealing outside the rigidities of diplomatic channels. The British, you know, had a complete misconception of Bobby Kennedy's trip to Malaysia. Luckily I was able to explain it to the Prime Minister. Our ambassador didn't know...."

All in the Family

Once when MacMillan & Company was about to bring out David Kahn's book, "The Code Breakers," a ranking American official became so carried way with the possible advantages of the Special Relationship that he proposed that Prime Minister

MacMillan be approached to "intervene with his family publishers on behalf both of the national interest and the family interest" in keeping Kahn's material classified.

A Useful Foreign Precedent?

When a former chairman of the British Joint Intelligence Committee was appointed UK ambassador to NATO, there was intramural suspicion that he carried with him, via his old contacts in London, readier access to more US intelligence than was available to his non-CIA colleague, the US ambassador to NATO. For certain members of the American intelligence community, such speculation provided much private pleasure, and hopes were expressed for emulation on this side of the Atlantic.

Our Neighbor to the North

In the early 1940s the octogenarian historian, Poultney Bigelow, when autographing his memoirs for a young TLH, inscribed: "Hoping for perpetual peace and reciprocity, at least between the US and Canada." Even this was threatened by Vietnam. In the mid-1960s, when the Canadians were deemed insufficiently supportive of US policy, Assistant Secretary of State Bill Bundy suggested that "Perhaps it's time to touch them up with a bit of brass." By this he meant cutting down on Ottawa's normal access to US intelligence "until they come around."

The Green Book

"Since 1930" the editors of the annual Washington Green book have considered themselves the arbiters of social position and usage. According to the staff, "people kill to get in."

The book still refuses the joint listing of unmarried live-togethers. The staff makes every effort, however, to respond to protocol questions. One of their most famous inquiries was from the widow who asked if she could dress her recently deceased husband in a tuxedo for a viewing that would be held before six p.m.

Those dropped from the Green Book "for cause" over the years include Sherman Adams, Ben Bradlee, Ramsay Clarke, William O. Douglas, Abe Fortas, Jean Harris, Alger Hiss, Wayne Hayes, Barbara Howar, Hamilton Jordan, Wilbur Mills, and John and Martha Mitchell.

★ ★ ★

VII

YOUTHFUL RETROSPECTIVES
★ ★ ★

Off to a Musical Career

Early in life, between ages 5-9, TLH was believed to have musical talents. In addition to his school and sports, he took piano lessons from Miss Ruth Gingles. His promising musical career ended when Miss Gingles married the local piano dealer and left town. She always claimed that her students were five degrees removed from Beethoven– she had studied under a student of a student of a student of Beethoven's.

While the departure of Miss Gingles cut short one possible professional career path, the piano persisted as a pleasurable lifelong pursuit. TLH still occasionally performs for friends on his Bechstein in the downstairs living room, or in the upstairs music room on Jane's Steinway. Jane's piano once belonged to Noel Coward. When he sold his Paris apartment after World War II, it came into the hands of her uncle, Drew Dudley, one of Noel's intimate friends. It was accompanied by a note that read: "Drew Darling, I remember that night in Cap d'Antibes. Noel."

As a junior high schooler, TLH privately played Chopin ballades. Publicly he provided the piano accompaniment for Mankato businessmen at their weekly Kiwanis club meetings, where they sang songs like 'Boost, boost, boost every builder." His last semi-public appearance was as one of a piano foursome playing the Champagne Tocatta at a turn of the century gathering in Washington on New Year's eve, 2000.

The Old Country Has Changed

Growing up with a Congregational and Episcopal church background, TLH was aware of his minority status. In Mankato the majority were Lutherans and Catholics. Scandinavian Lutherans were prominent, and his highly motivated, fourth grade teacher, Petra Lien, volunteered to teach Norwegian to the ten-year-old TLH during his lunch hour.

Until the 1930s it had been a local business practice to present a deserving retiree with a gold watch on retirement. Advanced thinkers in Mankato briefly decided to change this custom and, instead of the watch, to grant a retirement gift of a round trip ticket to modern Sweden. Unfortunately, the Swedish families of Southern Minnesota had retained the customs and values of the Sweden of the 1870s. The first awardees under the new policy came back to Mankato with horror stories about the embarrassingly socialist, sexually expanding, Sweden that they had encountered in their old age. There was a speedy return to the gold standard.

An Eventful 1936

When TLH was age 10, his father gave him Landon sunflower buttons to distribute in the schoolyard during Landon's campaign against FDR in the 1936 presidential race. At the same time the senior Hughes also demonstrated the fervor of his Republican convictions by deliberately climbing the post office steps, ostentatiously ignoring Postmaster General James Farley, who was there addressing a small group of Mankato Democrats.

On December 11, 1936, guests were invited to the Hughes home to celebrate TLH's eleventh birthday. Suddenly the festivities were halted, so that the group could hear the radio broadcast from London of King Edward VIII's abdication speech. The youngsters listened soberly as the king said that he could not continue without the support of the woman he loved. When he finished, the Mankato school superintendent, who was present, broke the silence with his verdict: "It will rank in history with the Gettysburg address."

Debate Opens Vistas

For TLH, four years of Midwestern high school debating opened visas to the outside world. Weekly tournaments in the nearby Dakotas, Wisconsin, and Iowa led to repeated victories and a growing reputation for the Mankato team. They participated in national student congresses in Lexington, Kentucky and Indianapolis, Indiana. After winning the Minnesota state debate championship, TLH went on to a national second place win in original oratory. Some judges' ballots survived from the Minnesota debates of 1940-3. Three of them showed Tom Hughes of Mankato defeating Walter Mondale of Elmore. Despite that, a friendly lifelong association ensued.

From Debate to Stalin's Daughter

John Zell, one of TLH's high school debate partners, later practiced psychiatry in Phoenix, Arizona. One day a new woman patient walked into his office. Her last name was Alliluyeva, and she thought she might need counseling. Zell asked her to tell him a bit about her previous life. She replied: "To begin with, I am Josef Stalin's daughter. How's that for starters?"

A Jump Start with Student Federalists

Clarence K. Streit's "Union Now" (1939) excited a young generation of student activists. The book proposed a postwar federal union of democracies. It linked the American federal experience with the need for a new world organization for peace. In high school in Scarsdale, New York, Harris Wofford took the lead. The future US Senator and president of Bryn Mawr College, then age 17, founded the first Student Federalist chapter in Scarsdale. TLH soon organized the second chapter in Mankato, and one of his favorite Minnesota debate colleagues, Emmy Lou Lindgren of South St Paul, quickly organized the third.

In a 1944 letter to TLH, Emmy Lou described the arrival at her high school of the glamorous young Wofford, whom she later married. Rain did not dampen the ardor, at least of the female Student Federalists. One of them seized a chance to tie one of Wofford's loose shoe laces, even though she had to kneel down in a mud puddle to do it. Emmy Lou reported that Harris calmly accepted this obeisance, and put his other foot forward after the first shoe had been tied.

As the student leaders campaigned for federal union, young romances flourished, subsided, and flourished again. Someday an enterprising graduate student will break into the Student Federalist correspondence files in the New York Public Library and be rewarded with the interplay of business and pleasure hidden in the Student Federalist saga.

★ ★ ★

At Close Quarters with History

At age 18, TLH succeeded Wofford as national president of Student Federalists. After a speaking tour of Eastern Canada and a nationwide broadcast on American Forum of the Air, he testified at the platform committees of both the Republican and Democratic conventions in 1944. A Look Magazine photographer followed him around for several days at the Republican meeting taking a memorable photo of him sharing a single seat with the ample Hedda Hopper, the social columnist known for her huge hats.

★ ★ ★

A Friendly Foursome

TLH spent some weeks in the summer of 1944 in Washington. He had a room at the Ontario Apartments, the residence of Clarence Streit. Among their close neighbors was a nationally famous radio broadcaster who had divorced his first two wives, and had then married a third. Putting first things first, however, the four of them remained seriously devoted to the bridge table. Apparently still on the best of terms, they made up a fearsome foursome at bridge that met regularly. TLH considered it a social arrangement without precedent at home in Southern Minnesota.

Glimpses of the Great

For TLH perhaps the biggest eye opener of his youth was attending the founding conference of the United Nations in San Francisco in 1945. Harold Stassen was there, home from the war, and preparing for a presidential bid in 1948. Many Student Federalists admired him. His assistant was Cord Meyer Jr., also just back from the war. He was soon to be elected President of United World Federalists, the parent organization with whom the Student Federalists were affiliated. The San Francisco conference was the first big world event near the war's end, and the cast of world leaders, foreign statesmen, and other eminent delegates was scintillating.

(The secretary of the UN Conference was Alger Hiss. The shadow of his brief presidency at the Carnegie Endowment three years later, and the furor over his trial and sentencing, had subsided by the time TLH became president of the Endowment in 1971.)

Overtaken by Events

During the UN conference in 1945, as a part of his Student Federalist presidential duties, TLH did some public speaking around the Bay Area. An international relations conference at Mills College proved to be especially memorable, not only because of the high quality of the daytime discussions, but for its instructive after hours activity as well. It turned out that the student leadership in California was precocious in more ways than one.

A day of intellectual arguments about the nature of the postwar world order had ended when the 18- year- old conference leader invited TLH to join her in an extra-curricular evening rendezvous. She was a Student Federalist, and she told TLH that his responsibility as national president was to support local SF activity every way he could. She led him to an outdoor amphitheater on the Mills campus. There, in a private hideaway, she soon made it clear that her abilities were not merely intellectual, nor were her enthusiasms limited to a postwar union of democracies. The experience certainly broadened TLH's personal horizons.

After a lengthy and enjoyable evening, his companion suggested that perhaps the next night TLH might like to participate in an expanded enterprise, by joining her again, along with two of her local Student Federalist boyfriends, to constitute a congenial federalist foursome. But TLH thought that this proposition pushed his presidential duties too far.

He backed away from the proposed four-way hookup, explaining that he really had to return to the UN conference to interview Molotov. "Too bad", she said. "The other boys are two of our most active Student Federalists. I had hoped to give you an inside glimpse of the vitality of our chapter here in the Bay Area." "Don't worry," TLH replied. "You already have."

Another Path Not Taken

Back at Carleton between federalist forays, TLH continued waiting on table to help pay his way through college. One Thanksgiving he was serving the dinner table of Mrs. Donald Cowling, the college president's wife. Dessert consisted of whole peach pies, wrapped in crust. When TLH collected the dessert plates, there was one peach stone per person, except for Mrs. Cowling.

After coffee, everything still seemed normal. When she departed, TLH and his fellow waiters looked around the area and found nothing. Mrs. Cowling never seemed any worse for wear, but the mystery of her missing peach stone was never resolved. Even so, the circumstances may have played a role in discouraging TLH from pursuing a waiter's career.

The Rhodes Experience: 1947-9

TLH arrived in England in September, 1947, to take up residence as a Rhodes Scholar at Balliol College, Oxford. Balliol was thought to be Oxford's most self-satisfied college. TLH was reminded of this daily as he sorted through the incoming "H" mail in the porter's lodge, where the small number of Hughes letters were always surrounded by an endless stream from famous Huxley graduates of Balliol addressed to the Huxley generation still in residence.

Balliol's 19th century master, Benjamin Jowett, declared that his purpose in life was "to inoculate the word with Balliol." He advised British viceroy-designates: "Never apologize. Never explain. Get it done and let them howl." The college historians considered Balliol men to be a distinct breed. One of them famously told a colleague that he once met a man who had met Napoleon "You could tell at once that Bonaparte was not a Balliol man."

Nothing Scientific About It

During his first week at Oxford, TLH enrolled in a graduate seminar with Professor G.D.H. Cole, then a prominent author of books like "The Intelligent Woman's Guide to the Postwar World." Cole quickly noticed that there were some Americans among the attendees. "Will any Americans here, who believe in social science, please raise their hands?" Three hands went up and Cole promptly said: "Out! Out! I don't want anybody here who thinks there is any such thing. We are dealing with social theory, not social science. There is nothing scientific about it." TLH was the only American who had not raised his hand and he was allowed to stay.

Debating English Style

TLH soon signed up to debate at the Oxford Union where an epigram easily outweighed the encyclopedia. A speedy adjustment was required. The US national debate topic the previous year had been a heavy one: "Resolved: that a federal world government should be established." That contrasted with the topics of TLH's first two debates at Oxford. The first was "Resolved: that this house thinks Columbus went too far." The second was: "Resolved: that this house deplores the fact that while woman first induced man to eat, he took to drinking all alone."

Harold Laski Explains

Harold Laski soon came up to Oxford to describe his recent visit to Moscow. "If only you could have seen the twinkle in Stalin's eye as he put me into his official chauffeur-driven car to take me back to my hotel…" A don sitting next to TLH said: "I was with that group. We were bussed around, and Laski never saw Stalin at all."

"But then, I also remember Laski's encounter with Marxist hecklers when he was here addressing a Labour Party meeting. When some in the audience began to heckle the hecklers, Laski admonished them: 'Leave them alone. After all, we are all followers of Marx—they in their way, I in his.'"

Italian Attractions

The first professorial lecture attended by TLH featured A. J. P. Taylor at the Sheldonian Theatre. He began speaking as he walked down the aisle to the podium. Passing TLH he was saying: "You must always bear in mind that the chief object of each of the great powers before the first World War was to make sure that Italy was on the other side when the war began." Others, subsequently, would echo this theme. Henry Kissinger later pronounced: "The Italian contribution is complete when we land at Ciampino airport in Rome." An American ambassador once said he had been "out to see the Italian navy, fortunately through a glass bottomed boat."

TLH nevertheless found Italy irresistible, and he spent the spring vacation of 1948 there during the historic Italian elections. In many ways it was a contest between the communists and the CIA. In Rome and Milan visible young Americans, like TLH and his friend from Oxford, Tim Atkeson, were immediately suspected of being on the CIA payroll. That was untrue, but the CIA did bankroll dozens of vivid political posters that were plastered each morning on any available wall space. The communist posters featured imperialist Uncle Sam performing a variety of grizzly deeds. The CIA's Christian Democratic posters featured happy family groups, contrasted with a glowering Josef Stalin endorsing "free love." The Oxonians collected an assortment of posters for their college rooms. The Library of Congress later asked TLH for his, "since the CIA is so much a part of the American way of life."

Armed with letters of introduction from friends, the young Americans never knew quite what to expect. At a tea dance in Rome they found themselves mingling with young ex-Fascist officers who, not long before, had seen service in Russia. On the beach near Pisa, the visitors helped locals remove the World War II barbed wire.

One night in Milan they splurged to buy tickets for La Scala. It was the first postwar performance of Kirstin Flagstad in Tristan and Isolde. A family friend had a bit part in the production, and asked to meet them at the conclusion of Act

Two. His own role was finished at that point, and before they knew it, they were driving to Menton on the Riviera. Their host assumed they had just come to hear him, never mind the famous Norwegian diva.

Lady Astor

When Lady Astor was a guest at the Oxford Union, she too had just returned from Moscow. But her experience contrasted with Laski's. "I asked Stalin when he was going to end the Czarist regime, and the translator fainted." Later the Rhodes scholars were invited down to Cliveden, the Astor's famous country house. It had been the center of the appeasement set in the 1930s, but guests were too polite to bring that up. Originally Lady Astor was a Virginian. She said she had never known how proud she was of her background until she saw "Gone with the Wind."

Prewar Anglo-German Protocol

Stories of prewar Oxford abounded. Elvis Stahr, later Secretary of the Army in the Kennedy administration, once told TLH about the Rhodes banquets of 1937 and 1938. In those pre-war years there were still German Rhodes scholars in residence. Thus in 1937 the three toasts were to the King, to the President of the United States, and to the Chancellor of the German Reich. A quarter of the room remained seated for the latter toast, and the Rhodes trustees were consumed with embarrassment over this discourtesy.

Many of the then trustees were cut from the mold of Lord Halifax of appeasement fame, who had once been quoted as saying: "I often think how much easier the world would have been to manage if Herr Hitler and Signor Mussolini had chanced to have been at Oxford." In any event the trustees had an urgent meeting to discuss how they could avoid a similar unpleasantness at the 1938 dinner. In their wisdom, they decided that next time they would combine the toasts to the American president and the German chancellor.

So at the 1938 banquet, just after Munich, everybody stood up for the toast "To the King." The next toast was "To the President of the United States and the Chancellor of the German Reich." Half of the room refused to rise this time, including Elvis Stahr. Thereupon a crusty old trustee, sitting next to him, put a hand on his shoulder and said: "Good for you, young man! I wouldn't stand up for that Franklin D. Roosevelt either!"

Choose What You Like, Professor

There were still stories told about earlier royals for the amusement of Americans. The future King George V as a young man—all his life for that matter—had tastes that ran to sea-going and stamp collection, rather than the serious discipline that goes into learning a foreign language. Thus despite his German antecedents, he was vexed by the constant corrections of his German tutor. He was said to have exploded one day: "Der, die, or das Sommer is really very hot today. Choose what you like, Professor."

England's Greatest Queen

David Webster of the BBC was fond of telling about the christening of the Queen Mary, the ocean liner, in the 1930s. The name for the new ship was to have been the Queen Victoria. King George V, however, was present at the Savoy Hotel when the head of the Cunard Line rose to speak. He said how proud Cunard was that "our splendid new ship will be named for England's greatest queen." Quicker to his feet than usual, King George immediately jumped up and said: "Oh, my wife will be so pleased." Queen Victoria instantly gave way to Queen Mary.

Once in looking over Foreign Office Records, TLH actually came across marginal notations on a document where George V had written: "A very interesting memorandum. I have read it—not all of it, of course. G. R."

Windsor Castle in the Dark

Back in the 1940s, a well-known British artist was commissioned by the palace authorities to paint Windsor Castle and its environs. This particular artist was known for his dark hues, especially his shades of brown. The day came for a presentation of the completed picture to King George VI, and the king looked at it silently for a while. Then he said: "Pity you had such bloody awful weather."

From Oxford to Argyleshire

Lavish hospitality schemes in England, Scotland, Wales, and Ireland were laid on for Rhodes men during Oxford's long vacations between terms. TLH recalls weekends at great houses with hunt balls, gala dinners, and much hilarity. At a Christmas-time service in a rural church in Argyleshire, the local choir attempted Haydn's "Creation". Spinsters on their side of the transept sang: "For unto us child is born." Gentlemen songsters opposite, dressed in kilts, responded with: "Wonderful! Wonderful!"

The Order of the Thistle

TLH bicycled from Oxford to Edinburgh in 1948. King George VI and his family happened to be there en route to Balmoral. At an Order of the Thistle service in St. Giles Cathedral, all eyes were on the royals as they took their places before the choir. After crossing the River Tweed, the English monarch was supposed to cease being head of the Anglican church of England to become head of the Presbyterian church of Scotland. Testing the seriousness of this transition, the canny Scots had chosen well-known hymns that had the same music as in England but different verses in Scotland. King George finally had to put on his glasses to accommodate the unfamiliar verses, and the expected titters swept through the Scottish pews.

A Display of Scottish Ingenuity

TLH visited the Scottish birthplace of his great-grandfather Lowe in Kurriemuir/Cortachy, then in Forfarshire. Looking for better farmland, he emigrated to Canada in the 1830s and then to Minnesota following the Civil War. After half a century of experimenting in international living, he took out his US citizenship papers in 1885.

However, he quickly wrote an apologetic letter to Queen Victoria at Windsor Castle. Frugal in both soul and purse, and inspired by Scottish ingenuity, he informed her that while he had technically pledged allegiance to President Cleveland, he didn't really mean it. And, by the way, could she kindly spare him a few pounds sterling to carry him through the next planting season?

★ ★ ★

Spoonerisms

Undergraduates at Oxford were still making up Spoonerisms in honor of the Rev. William Archibald Spooner, Warden of New College in the 1870s. He was fondly remembered for his malapropisms and mangled sentences. For example, on announcing the hymn in the college chapel: "Kinquering Congs their titles take." Or his patriotic toast to Queen Victoria: "Three cheers for our queer old dean." Or his dismissal of a student: "You have deliberately tasted two worms, and you can leave Oxford by the first town drain." Or his revisionist instructions from the pulpit of New College chapel: "In the sermon I have just preached, whenever I said Aristotle, I meant St. Paul."

Spooner was run a close second by Maurice Bowra, a 20th century warden of Wadham. In his Christmas letter to graduates he once wrote: "The Master of Balliol has been ill, but unfortunately is getting better. Otherwise deaths have been poor for this time of year.

Other Prominent Men

There was a famous encounter in the 1920s between Sir Herbert Warren, then President of Magdelen College, and a new undergraduate, Prince Chichibu, the second son of the Emperor of Japan. During the matriculation audience that the President granted to all new Magdelen men, there was the usual amount of genteel fencing, marked by awkward pauses.

Finally Sir Herbert bluntly inquired: "Where did you get an odd name like Chichibu? What would that be in English?" The Japanese prince deferentially mentioned that people had Japanese names in Japan, not all of which were easily translatable. However, if an English equivalent were insisted upon, he supposed that Chichibu could roughly be rendered as "son of God." There was another lengthy pause while the President of Magdalen reflected. "Young man," he said thoughtfully, "I have no doubt that, in due course, you will find the sons of many other prominent men in residence in the college."

★ ★ ★

How are Things at Jesus?

How are things at Jesus? Welsh relatives in Cardiganshire assumed that a Hughes would be enrolled at Jesus College, the

217

Welsh college at Oxford, and not at Balliol, the Scots college. But once they were reconciled to that anomaly, TLH had memorable visits to Wales.

Tredegar, Monmouthshire, was a hot bed of leftwing sentiment. The town clock in the city center had been painted red the night of the Labour Party victory in 1945. The "Little Lenin library" shelves in the local athenaeum showed evidence of frequent use. Aneuran "Nye" Bevan, the local MP, had just become Housing Minister in London. ("That's too big a job for my Nye, just too big," his aging mother said, as she rocked in her rocking chair when her neighbors took TLH in to meet her.)

Visits to local coal mines alternated with concerts in Cardiff. One evening in Wales a conversation with a rather deaf old neighbor lasted five minutes, before TLH discovered that the neighbor was complaining about Russians while TLH was talking about rations.

Comfortable Labourites

Then there was the weekend retreat with thirty Oxford socialists at the Berkshire estate of Lord Faringdon, a Labour peer. For three days the Oxonians roamed around his eighteenth century house, set amid acres of trees and fountains, formal gardens, statuary, outdoor theater, swimming pool, etc. Discussions were held under rows of van Dykes and Renoldses. The students slept in four-poster beds, dreaming of the classless society. TLH thought that this was not the way the left wing of the Farmer-Labor party in Minnesota demonstrated the fervor of its class consciousness. However a visit to the annual Labour party conference at the grimy, kitschy seaside resort of Blackpool soon restored a sense of proportion.

Endorsing Truman

Lord Lindsay, the-soon-to-retire master of Balliol, was TLH's tutor for his first term at Oxford. Lindsay was a Labour lord, but his wife, also a confirmed socialist, resented titles and insisted on being called "Mrs. Lindsay." So they were introduced as Lord and Mrs Lindsay. On a November day in 1948, Mrs. Lindsay interrupted a tutorial and announced: "The BBC is on the phone." As the master rose to take the call, his wife said: "Oh, no, Sandy. It's not for you. It's for Mr. Hughes."

The BBC sounded desperate. "We hope you can help us. We are airing a program on the American election tomorrow night, and we have been scouring all of Britain to find someone who supports President Truman. The Chicago Tribune chief in London will speak for Governor Dewey, and a Negro from the cast of Anna Lucasta will speak for Henry Wallace. But we can't find anyone to speak for President Truman. Someone told us that there was a person named Hughes at Balliol who might possibly be willing to do this. We could send a car to fetch you and bring you to London. At the Alexandra Palace we'll feed you well, ply you with port, and put you on the telly." "That sounds terrific. Of course, I'd be delighted to support President Truman."

The next day TLH was whisked off to London by chauffeur-driven car for his baptism with television, then in its primitive stages. The next day Oxford friends told him that, after his considerable wining and dining, he had begun by saying: "American voters are about to choose between Dewey and Truman, two of the least seductive personalities in American public life. But given that choice, you would have to pick Truman." Not exactly the endorsement to end all endorsements, but the BBC seemed grateful.

★ ★ ★

A Word for Victor Gollancz

One night at Oxford TLH was in a group that had dinner with Victor Gollancz, a celebrated English author, who was then at work on a biography of one of the mistresses of King Edward VII. Gollancz had decided on a workable precis for his book, but was still searching for a critically missing verb. "At the palace she regularly presided over private functions, and she frequently _____ the royal balls." After a heated discussion, a consensus was reached that "arranged" would be suitable, and Gollancz accepted it as the perfect solution.

★ ★ ★

US Presidents and their Honorary Degrees

Robin Nisbet roomed with TLH his first year at Balliol. When they met again at Oxford in 1996, Robin had become the Corpus Professor of Latin. He shared an unofficial draft, submitted for the University Orator's use when President Clinton came for an honorary degree. There were some splendid lines:
"WILHELMUS JEFFERSONIUS AIRPLANUS

CLINTONENSIS, SALUTAMUS VENERABILIS
UNIVERSITATIS OXONIENSIS. QUONDAM RHODUS
SCHOLASTICUS ET MARIJUANA NON-
INHALIENSIS ET
EX BELLO VIETNAMENSIS NOT CONSCRIPTIONE
EXCUSATUS. SUBSEQUENTIS GUBERNATOR
RESPUBLICA ARKANSENSIS ET PERPETRATOR
CRIMINALIS SLEAZISIMUS IN NOMINE 'AQUA
BLANCA' SCANDALUS, CUM TUA UXORE
HILLARIUS
RODDAMA CLINTESTERONE. ETIAM
LEGOVERNUS
MULTITUDINIS CUM ULTAE BIMBONES, GENNIFA
FLORES, PAULA JONES ET CETERA, ET CETERA.
SATYRIASIS ABNORMALIS IN MDO PREIDENTIUS
KENNEDENSIS. TUA FAMA EXTENDID PER OMNE
MUNDO PRO JOGGENDO, JUVANDO AD
SAXOPHONIUM
ET NON MUCH ELSE. ESPERAMOS QUID PRO QUO
MULTI RICHI AMERICANI DONABUNT MUCHOS
DOLLARES AD NIVRSITATEM OXONIENSIS.

OMNES; VIVAT, VIVAT CLINTSTONE YABA-DABA-
DOO.

(In the real ceremony for Clinton, this salute was toned down.)

★ ★ ★

There was a tradition for honoring American presidents
at Oxford. When Harry Truman came to get his honorary
degree, an undergraduate had leaned out of a Hertford College

window to yell at the procession en route to the Shedonian Theatre: "Give 'em hell, Harricum!"

Glimpses of the Foreign Office

Historic lore from the British Foreign Office provided grist for amusement at Oxford high tables. One story mixed horse racing and diplomacy with the summer of 1914. The great Arc de Triumphe race was being held on the Continent, and the Foreign Office was naturally alert for the returns. Suddenly the wireless started to spell out: "A-R-C-H-D-U-K-E-F-E-R-D-I-N-A-N-D-S-A-R-A-J-E-V-O." By Jove, the Foreign Office code clerk exclaimed, "not a British horse among the first three."

A second involved that ancient retiree from the Research Department of the Foreign Office who reputedly said, after serving from 1905 to 1950: "Year after year the fretters and worriers would come to me with awful predictions of the outbreak of war. I denied it each time. I was only wrong twice."

Preserving the War Office

Sir Austen Chamberlain's 1935 memoirs tell of a conversation with Herbert Asquith when he was Chancellor of the Exchequer before the first world war. Asquith had before him a proposal for the construction of an underground passage from the War Office to the Horse Guards, with cellars where papers might be stored, and work carried on, in case of aerial attack. On the proposal the chief civil servant of the day, Sir George Murray, had minuted: "This may be safely turned down. No sane enemy, acquainted with our institutions, would destroy the War Office."

★ ★ ★

A Beneficiary of the British National Health Service.

While he was at Oxford TLH had a girlfriend from Sweet Briar who was spending her junior year in Paris. They had arranged to meet on a train at Waterloo Station in London for a trip to Devon. As the train began to move, TLH discovered that his companion was still on the platform. So, clinging to the baggage, he jumped off the moving train and skinned his knee in the process. Sirens wailed. An ambulance, nurses, and photographers quickly arrived. Pictures on the front pages of papers the next day were captioned: "National Health Service treats American patient at Waterloo."

★ ★ ★

Cross-Channel Collaboration

TLH's Sweet Briar-Oxford collaboration in 1948-9 was an extended one. On the English side of the channel there were Oxford boat races, dances, and other social events. There were visits to London, to Blenheim, to Stratford-upon-Avon, and seaside trips to Devonshire and Wales. On the French side of the channel there was Paris itself, a conference in Luxemburg, Christmas in Zurich, and New Year's eve at Zuers, an alpine ski resort then in the French Zone in Austria. The chimney sweeps swept out the old year by dancing with the women guests, and everybody drank toasts "to a speedy Austrian peace treaty."

Parisian Memories

Introduced to Paris under these romantic circumstances, TLH had many return visits. His cousin, Dr. William Lowe Mundy, served in the late 1940s on the medical staff at the American Hospital of Paris in Neuilly. He was regularly summoned by the Duke of Windsor to administer sedatives to the Duchess so she could get a full morning's sleep in advance of her exhausting afternoon and evening schedules.

TLH and Jean had first met Bob and Sylvia Blake in 1959 when Bob served in the US Embassy in Tunisia. Ten years later Bob was DCM in Paris when TLH was DCM in London, and they could now share lessons on the handling of ambassadors.

173 Boulevard St. Germain

While in Paris for a conference in the 1970s, TLH found himself one day on the Boulevard St. Germain. He stopped by number 173, the Carnegie Endowment's former European headquarters. Almost directly across the street was the famous Café de Flore, where Hemingway, Fitzgerald, and the rest of the American expatriates of the 1920s could, if they wished, gaze upon the Endowment's mansion and speculate what went on for peace behind its walls. According to the guard at the doorway, the place was known on the left bank as "la maison du high life pacifique."

Nicholas Miraculous

Some Endowment officials like President Nicholas Murray Butler had enjoyed summering at the Carnegie building in Paris in the 1920s and 1930s. The rest of the year, "Nicholas Miraculous" spent most of his time being President of Columbia University. But he was always available for a public speech. Indeed he was known far and wide for his readiness at speechmaking. The press reported that he had a brass pole in his New York City house, and that he slid down it immediately upon receiving the slightest intimation that there was an unoccupied rostrum within the city limits. Reputedly he had a similar pole in Paris.

An Alumnus Returns

With the German occupation in 1940, the Carnegie officials departed, leaving the building in charge of Madame Perroux, the long- time secretary-administrator in Paris. From time to time, during the first year or two under the Nazis, there would be knocks on the front door. Each time she feared for the worse, but nothing serious happened.

Finally, in late 1942, a German colonel appeared in full uniform. Madame Perroux was certain this meant the end. He sauntered in, placed his cap on a library table, and said: "I had a Carnegie fellowship here a dozen years ago. It has taken me quite a while, and much effort. But now I am in charge of this arrondissement. Please relax. You no longer have anything to fear. I have nothing but pleasant memories of this building, and of my time with the people in it."

Tracing Steps

In the 1980s, TLH inherited from the Edward S. Hughes estate a number of French paintings and prints, including a Vuillard. Ned's original invoices from postwar Paris guided TLH for a memorable few days as he traced his late cousin's footsteps around the left bank art and antique shops where he had made his purchases. The collection was later donated to the French-American Foundation in New York.

Embracing Minnesota Populism

As a high school freshman, TLH had taken the then-famous Minnesota multi-phasic test at the state university, and, to the consternation of some of his family friends, he scored "especially high" in his egalitarian social consciousness.

An Israeli Kibbutz Sets Limits

During summer vacation from law school in 1950, TLH joined a group of young volunteers who lived and worked on a village commune in Israel. The kibbutz was Ein Hashofet, "Spring of the Judge", named for Justice Brandeis. It was located in the Emek valley, the heartland of the Old Testament and the site of Armageddon. The Korean War had just begun, and the kibbutzniks repeatedly made clear their opposition to "American imperialism." While the radio broadcast news of daily American military setbacks, the volunteers worked with the kibbutzniks, clearing stones, sifting dirt, and picking plums. Socialist austerity was said to promote a new, and promising, egalitarian way of life–in contrast to "the America of Paul Robeson."

After a day of hard labor, there were night-time intellectual tasks. TLH was assigned to observe decision-making. Did the kibbutzniks talk themselves into unanimity, as they said, or simply get tired arguing? This was a Mapam kibbutz, directly linked to that Israeli socialist party, and the summer's experience set limits to TLH's left-wing instincts.

The kibbutz leadership unhesitatingly favored indoctrination. As the liaison officer said: "If we don't indoctrinate our kids, someone else will. The Jesuits were right you know. They may have been unscrupulous, but they were educationally correct. We teach our children the gospel of the struggle. Dissention would wreck kibbutz solidarity. Diverse political views are not represented in our classrooms before age 16—"until the children are old enough to see that the other positions are wrong."

The kibbutz library displayed Mapam party books and periodicals. The only English language material was the "New Times" from Moscow. It tended to feature colored photos of Stalin on its covers—"the name on the parched lips of the Negro in Tennessee."

★ ★ ★

For Liberal Read Fascist Throughout

Before leaving at the end of August, 1950, the volunteers were asked to sum up their impressions at a kibbutz meting. While praising their many impressive achievements and wishing them well, TLH courted controversy. "Given a choice between a closed, dogmatic, partisan society and an open, skeptical, liberal one, I still would have no problem in choosing the second." Challenging his ideological audience, he glanced at the photo of Justice Brandeis on the wall and concluded: "The eminent judge up there would, I believe, choose the same way." Many kibbutzniks quickly offered their sympathy to several of TLH's colleagues for their having had to suffer this "neo-fascist" in their group.

★ ★ ★

Growing Up and Getting Ready

While still in Israel the group met with Martin Buber in Jerusalem, who challenged them by asking "Are you ready? Are you ready to play your role— in the world, in history?" Not sure how to answer that question, the group went on to Eilat. That gave TLH the opportunity to do his bit for Israel by standing armed guard duty against "Arab marauders" in the Negev, a realistic foretaste of things to come.

★ ★ ★

Some Populism Still Lingered

Two years later, during the summer of 1952 after his graduation from law school and admission to the Minnesota bar, TLH joined his father's law firm in taking a local pro bono legal case. In Minnesota there was a homestead exemption from local property taxes. The issue was whether this exemption extended to rents received on homestead property, when the owner no longer resided there. "Wilson vs. the First National Bank of Mankato" became a celebrated case.

Exhibiting his socially conscious legal training at Yale, where "creditor's rights" was called "debtor's estates," TLH prepared the brief. It was filed with Judge Mason, a conservative friend of the bank and a social friend of the Hughes family. The judge took much longer than usual to consider the matter. Finally, to the bank's surprise and chagrin, he decided for the plaintiff. The bank immediately appealed to the Minnesota Supreme Court. Astonishingly enough, after weeks of deliberation, they agreed with Judge Mason. The rents were exempt, and the decision entered the law books as a high watermark of Minnesota legal populism.

VIII

ANECDOTAL ODDS AND ENDS
★ ★ ★

A Modest Foundation

The week that TLH became president of the Carnegie Endowment for International Peace, he received a postcard that read: "Mr. Hughes: What hast thou to do with peace? Kings IX -18." It would not be the last time that this question would be raised.

Decades of lackluster financial management by establishment bankers had left the peace endowment still a comparatively modest enterprise. It was not to be compared with the Ford or Rockefeller foundations, which were often described as large bodies of money surrounded by outstretched hands. Carnegie was a medium-sized endowment, like Zsa Zsa Gabor's. As she once said: "What I call loaded, I'm not. What others call loaded, I am."

Nomenclature

At the beginning of his presidency in the 1920s, Nicholas Murray Butler tried to take Peace out of the Endowment's title and call it the Carnegie International Endowment instead. He had the clairvoyance to anticipate Alfred North Whitehead's later warning that "the deliberate aim at Peace very easily passes into its bastard substitute, Anesthesia." In the 1970s when the computer spell checker arrived on the scene, it too had trouble with the Endowment's name. In this case the problem was with "Carnegie," and the computer suggested that it might be replaced with "carnage."

Internship Applications

A sampling of the annual applications for internships at the Endowment is worth preserving:

"I am presently a self-surviving student of political science hoping to make a career in the diplomatic corps. Meanwhile, are there any programs under your endowment plan that might assist a young woman like me with a stipend and field of action by which I may broaden and sharpen my pragmatic opportunities?"

"My thesis is that government officials opposed to arms control are haunted by their experience of child abuse. I would like to explore this theory in a practical way under your roof."

"My four years at Susquehanna University were pointed toward helping mankind get out of its present morass...Do you have anything available for a soon-to-be college graduate, who is a self-starter, and is not afraid to get things done? Yet who will respect and abide by the principles that have made your organization so great, and of which he eventually hopes to become President?"

A Higher Level Applicant

"Is this Tom Hughes of the Peace Endowment? This is Congressman Charlie Wilson from Texas, Tom. Just call me Charlie. I'm callin' about Speaker Jim (Congressman Jim Wright, who was being forced to resign as Speaker of the House for some minor infraction in 1989.) Now Speaker Jim has been for peace for many years, and I'd like to bring the two of you together productively. I think Jim might even have a future at the Peace Endowment. Of course, as you probably know, I myself am usually for war. But Speaker Jim and I are both from Texas."

"I should warn you, Charlie, that we are not trying to hire celebrities here at the Endowment. We are not looking for the Henry Kissingers and the Jeanne Kirkpatricks. Instead, we hire younger experts for shorter periods of time—people like Richard Holbrooke, Tony Lake, Pauline Baker, Bill Maynes, Jenonne Walker, Don McHenry, Doris Meissner, and Leslie Gelb—newcomers with rising talents, like them. Somehow I'm afraid that Speaker Jim is just too important a man to fit into our Carnegie matrix." "Oh, let's not judge anything in advance,

Tom. You come and have lunch with Speaker Jim and me at the Monocle on Capitol Hill next Wednesday noon."

On Wednesday, TLH arrived first and was ushered, ceremoniously, to Charlie Wilson's usual table. Charlie arrived next, in a sunny and expansive mood, kissing his way through table after table, and then detouring for waitresses in the kitchen. Once reaching his own table and TLH, Charlie began proclaiming his love for Pakistan, where he and his girlfriends were frequent visitors.

"Charlie, how did you come to have such a strong affinity for Pakistan?" "Now let me tell you, Tom. One morning I was shaving. I looked into the mirror, and I asked myself: Charlie Wilson what can you do to do in the Nehrus? Tom, I just can't stand the Nehrus. Now I know that some of you at Carnegie, like Selig Harrison, are in love with the Nehrus. As for me, whenever I get a chance, I shove it to the Nehrus. I detest them, everything about them.

"Suddenly it occurred to me. Charlie, you should cozy up to Pakistan. That'll be sure to set the Nehrus on edge. I went straight to the Pak embassy, and I told the doorman that I was worth a lot in potential aid for Pakistan. I quickly met one embassy officer after another. Soon I was in the ambassador's office. I explained that I was chairman of the subcommittee on appropriations, and that I could deliver untold millions of dollars in aid to Pakistan. They were suddenly very interested. They still are."

At that point Speaker Jim arrived. He had survived a lachrymose procession through the restaurant. As he moved along the tables of lunching Congressmen, there were sympathetic murmurs from all sides. "Sorry to hear about it Jim. Jim, if you ever need any help of any kind, please don't hesitate to call. I'm as near as your nearest phone." And so forth.

Joining us, the Speaker remembered that he and TLH had once been Air Force Reserve colleagues. He regretted that the 9999th squadron had been disbanded. Then getting right down to business, Jim allowed as how he had been offered office space at TCU (Texas Christian University). "That sounds like a good opportunity," said TLH hopefully. "But Mrs. Wright is minded to stay right here in Washington." "Well, Jim, I certainly wish we could accommodate you and Mrs. Wright, but I really think we are ill equipped to do so. You are such eminent people."

A Private Foreign Policy

In 1983, when the Carnegie Endowment closed its New York offices, there remained a mysterious safe for which nobody had a key. Finally it was dynamited open, and out tumbled a series of "Green Papers" marked "Top Secret: Butler Eyes Only". They turned out to be reports from around the world, sent by Endowment agents to President Nicholas Murray Butler. In the 1920s and 1930s, consistent with his imperial view of things, "Nicholas Miraculous" saw fit to classify them as part of his own little empire.

Irresistible Invitations

When Jacksonville University asked TLH to speak, they said they were "looking for someone who has both a strategic and humanistic view on how to achieve peace, and you are the only such person we have been able to find." Under the circumstances it was hard to say no.

In the 1920s the Carnegie Endowment contracted with Sigmund Freud for him to produce a study on "The Psychological Dimensions of War." Months later, he confessed to having a 'mental block" on the subject. Freud broke the contract and returned his fee.

"As Dr. Kwame Nkrumah said on arriving in Peking and learning that he had been overthrown as President of Ghana, 'I am happy to be here'." (TLH speaking to an Aerospace Industries meeting in Williamsburg, Virginia. 1966.)

Adding to a Stasi File

TLH paid several visits to East Germany in the 1970s and 80s, presumably expanding his Stasi file, trip after trip. In 1989 just before the fall of the Berlin Wall, he was invited to talk to a seminar of the Policy Planning Council of the Foreign Office in East Berlin. After the seminar, the director of the then International Relations Institute in Babelsburg, Potsdam, invited TLH to dinner at the Restaurant Ganymede.

There they were joined by a muscular woman with a notebook. She took copious notes for a couple of hours during dinner. Suddenly, at 9:00 p.m., she closed her notebook and announced: "This has been a fascinating discussion, gentlemen, but it must now cease. I must go to my swimming practice for the Olympics."

Later that night TLH went into the telephone operators' room at his East Berlin hotel and tried to place a call to West

Berlin. The connection took considerable time, effort, and ingenuity, but it was finally arranged by using circuits through Africa.

The English View the Germans

The English have a decent respect for history that can override their strongest wartime antagonisms. Thus the Examination Schools at Oxford still display a large pre-World War I portrait of Kaiser Wilhelm II, dressed in his scarlet doctoral robes and dating from the early 1900s when Oxford awarded him an honorary degree. Some said his fiercely upturned moustaches were intended to frighten those sitting for exams. But he was not fond of German socialists, and when Willy Brandt came to Oxford and spoke, with Wilhelm in the background, the juxtaposition did create an incongruous spectacle.

At University College, Oxford, in the 1980s, the wife of the college president, Lady Goodhart, was presiding over an afternoon tea. She opened by saying: "Of course, Mr. Hughes, I do not pretend to be an expert on foreign affairs. But I must say, I do take such satisfaction out of the continued division of Germany, don't you?"

In the 1990s, after German reunification, TLH and his wife Jane were in Halle-an-der-Salle visiting Handel's house. It was full of English visitors who naturally were surprised to learn that Handel was not entirely an Englishman. Jane had been listening to Berlitz cassettes to pick up useful German expressions. Reaching the exit simultaneously with an English pair, she said in a matter-of-fact manner "Entschuldigen, bitte" and magnanimously motioned for them to proceed ahead. Whereupon, Beatrice turned to Nigel, saying: "Nigel, the Germans are becoming so polite!"

★ ★ ★

Georgetown Seeks a Deduction

TLH had many connections with the dazzling Marietta Peabody Tree—as well as with Desmond Fitzgerald, her first husband, and with Ditchley House in England, an estate once owned by her second husband Ronald Tree. TLH and Jean had visited the Trees in Italy at their marvelous villa in Florence. There were also occasional dinner parties in New York hosted by Marietta and her friend, Kitty Carlisle Hart.

Shortly after the death of Ronnie Tree, TLH's secretary at Carnegie came in to say that Ambassador David Bruce had phoned requesting an appointment. In due course he arrived, accompanied by three reigning Georgetown ladies—Polly Fritchey, Susan Mary Alsop, and Oatsie Charles. "To what do I owe the honor of such an auspicious visit?" "It's about Ronnie Tree," the ambassador began.

"We are all Ronnie's friends, and we want to do something suitable in his memory. Just talking among ourselves, we think that we could raise a sum as high as $10,000, provided, of course, that we could claim a tax deduction. We thought you might have a suggestion about how we should proceed. Doing something in Ronnie's honor in his beloved Barbados might be preferable, but, of course, that is outside US jurisdiction.

"Well, if you are thinking of Barbados, maybe you should work through one of the Caribbean related foundations. How about the Royal Oak Foundation? They restore old properties, which sounds like something Ronnie would like." "But could we get a US tax deduction for it?" Bruce persisted. "Yes, I think they can arrange it. They know the way—'friends of', etc." "Oh, that's wonderful, Tom. Thanks so much. Just the suggestion we needed." They happily departed, and the Royal Oak people did indeed rescue the Georgetown luminaries from the onus of paying taxes.

A Surprise Encounter

Sometimes NGO circles had their own inside humor. In the 1970s and 80s, Waldemar Nielsen was a prominent and well informed critic of the foundation world. He decided to take on the new management of the Rockefeller Foundation, particularly Richard Lyman, who had succeeded John Knowles as president. Nielson composed a lengthy manuscript, detailing what he considered to be the unimaginative and maladroit aspects of the Lyman regime.

Being politically adept in the often competitive and retributive world of NGO executives, Nielson thought that, in fairness, he should show the draft manuscript to the Rockefeller president before publication. In doing so, he told Lyman that he hoped that he would point out any actual errors in the draft, as well as suggest deletions or amendments to anything Lyman consider unfair. To his surprise, the manuscript was returned without complaint or comment. So off it went to the publishers.

One evening some weeks later, Nielson saw Richard Lyman and "Jing," his formidable wife, approaching him determinedly during an intermission at the opera at Lincoln Center. "Wally Nielson! I have words for you!" Jing shouted. Nielson feared that retaliation was finally coming. Instead: "I just want you to know that I read that manuscript of yours! I agreed with it completely! It confirmed what I have always said—that Richard is a lousy administrator, entirely too pedestrian and ineffectual. You hit the nail right on the head! It certainly needed saying! I congratulate you, Wally!" Richard seemed to be smiling in long-suffering agreement.

Volkswagon Passengers

Hans-Adam, Prince of Liechtenstein, was the guest of honor at a stag dinner at Roger Kennedy's in Virginia. When the party broke up, Roger inquired whether anyone could drive the prince back to Georgetown. In the absence of any other volunteers, TLH offered a ride in his VW, and the prince accepted. Their destination was Claiborne Pell's house in Georgetown. Once there, the prince said he would just go in and check to be sure the King of Greece had left. He had, so all was in order.

A more problematical VW passenger was Ken Galbraith, the exceedingly tall Harvard professor and former ambassador to India. He asked whether it was a sunroof model. Fortunately it was. His head emerged a bit above roof-top.

Keeping Up with the Times

In January, 2006, Jane's daughter Alexandra Kuczynski took her mother on a shopping trip that she planned to write up for her weekly column in the New York Times. A shop on the west side was recommended by a fashion expert who told them that good dressing begins with the correct brassiere. Sure enough, the sales person suggested a larger bra size for Alexandra's mother.

Jane was still in New York when the Times published the details of their successful expedition. The column appeared the same day as a Carnegie trustees meeting in Washington. When TLH entered the room at Carnegie, a spontaneous storm of applause broke out. All the trustees, from the head of the Securities and Exchange Commission to the president of Princeton, seemed to have read Alexandra's article. TLH thanked them cordially for their interest, and said it was exceeded only by the telephone call he had had that morning from Jane's former husband's divorce lawyer who had also called with his congratulations.

★ ★ ★

With Renewed Respect

Once at Neiman-Marcus, TLH and Jane found Stanley Marcus himself autographing his new book, "Minding the Store." They expressed surprise that he had time to come to Washington for such a petty task, and he replied: "Always autograph them. They can't return them that way."

TLH then reminded him of a famous George Bernard Shaw story. Shaw had autographed one of his books "To Lady Sutherland with the utmost respect." When he later found the book in a used bookstore, he bought it back and returned it to the original owner. A second, new, inscription read: "To Lady Sutherland, with renewed respect. GBS"

At least a book's longevity could be greater this way, avoiding S. J. Perlman's fate about his: "Conceived in need, written in passion, remaindered in toto."

★ ★ ★

Who's Winning in Virginia?

John Warner was already married to Elizabeth Taylor when he ran for the Senate in 1978. His opponent was a friend of TLH, Andrew Pickens Miller. John Chancellor was still at NBC News, and on election night TLH telephoned him to ask how the Virginia campaign was going. Chancellor said: "I'll check with our big prophecy board." Returning, he reported: "At the moment, the Taylor ticket is one breast ahead."

As a member of the Senate Armed Services Committee, Senator Warner himself made only a gradual adjustment to Pentagon-ese. "Flexible Response" was one of the sacred phrases in the NATO doctrinal repertoire. One Sunday morning on national TV, while the Senator was still familiarizing himself with the concept, the phrase came out: "The world is going to have to change a lot before we can forsake our time-tested doctrine of Flexible Responsibility."

★ ★ ★

Conversations at the Airport

In the summer of 2009, Jane and TLH were returning to
Washington after a family vacation in northern Minnesota. In
the airport waiting room, she noticed a faintly familiar person
sitting knee to knee with TLH. Could she take his picture
with her iPhone? He nodded, while continuing to talk on his.
When he finished, Jane said: "You do a pretty good Al Franken
imitation!" He replied: "That's what I gotta do!"

The Minnesota Supreme Court had just confirmed
Franken's 225- vote victory in the US Senate race. Various high
school students now came up to ask him to sign their school
annuals. One of them asked: "Senator, on what committees are
you going to serve?" Franken said "Oh, probably Pensions…"
"Pensions? Gee, that's cool."

Similar Backgrounds

The last dog in the Hughes family was a beagle named Tammy
Faye. She resembled the evangelist who had mascaraed eyes
and who cried on demand. Like her namesake, the dog proved
to be an ordeal. She would regularly escape her leash, dash
down Western Avenue, and cross Wisconsin to her favorite
filling station. The attendants there would tie her to a pump
and phone home with the message: "Tammy Faye is here
again." The ultimate conclusion was that a new home for
Tammy Faye was needed.

The local animal welfare league listed a lady in Bowie,
Maryland, who was looking for a beagle, and Tammy Faye
was taken out for an interview. "Now tell me all about Tammy

Faye," her putative new owner began. "Well, all we know for sure is that she's a Virginian. She deserted her husband and children in Fredericksburg, climbed under a fence, and headed straight north." "Sounds just like me," said the lady in Bowie. "I'll take her."

Degrees en Masse

While in India in1964, visiting Chester Bowles, who was then serving his second term as ambassador, TLH flew with him to Calcutta where Bowles was to deliver the commencement address at a mass graduation ceremony. Last on the program was the granting of degrees to a cast of thousands. The Vice Chancellor of the university rose to do the honors, and gazing out on the multitude and gesturing toward various large clumps of students, he shouted into the microphone: "By wirtue of the authority wested in me as Wice-Chancellor of this university, I hereby declare you B.A., B.S., B.Phil,– with two or three B.A.-failed."

An Emergency Wine Tasting

After Obama's inauguration in 2009, there was great uncertainty, and a long delay, in setting dates for visits of foreign leaders. One May morning TLH and Jane had an emergency call from their friend Beate Lindemann in Berlin. Chancellor Merkel's long-awaited visit had suddenly been arranged, with just days to go. Beate's foundation, Atlantik

Bruecke (Atlantic Bridge) was planning an award ceremony for Merkel at the Library of Congress. The menus had to be printed that afternoon and reliable assistance was urgently needed.

"Chris, our agent, will arrive at your doorstep in a few minutes. He will bring thirteen bottles of wine, four white, five sparkling white, and four red. You and Jane must taste each of them immediately, and choose the best for the Merkel reception, bearing in mind that the Library of Congress puts restrictions on where red wine may be consumed. Then you must phone us immediately with your recommendations. There is no time to lose. We depend upon you."

The emergency wine tasters reported back just in time, but both of them spent a more relaxed and inactive afternoon than usual.

Stop the Press

In the mid -1980s Dr. Russell Kirk lectured at the Heritage Foundation on "Edmund Burke and the Future of American Politics." A member of the Washington press corps phoned to inquire whether Mr. Burke would be available for interviews after the lecture.

A week later the Carnegie Endowment hosted a press luncheon for David Webster, formerly of the BBC. TLH received a letter from a reporter, regretting that he was not free to hear Mr. Daniel Webster.

A Phantom Photo

In the mid-1970s TLH was in Hong Kong for a "Williamsburg Meeting," an off-the-record conclave of invited American and Asian foreign policy types. It was an effort by John D. Rockefeller III to emulate for Asia what his brother David had done for Europe with his "Bilderburg Group." The Hong Kong Standard headlined the event: "VIP Group in Top Secret HK Meeting."

There was a large front page photo of TLH arriving with two Chinese bodyguards. The mischievous caption underneath read: "The first delegate to arrive identified himself as Mr. Rockefeller. Another Mr. Rockefeller arrived five minutes later. Neither Rockefeller would divulge details of the talks. Both referred questioners to Robert Barnett, vice president of an organization calling itself the Asia Society."

Barnett denied that there were two Rockefellers attending, and denied that there was anything secret, explaining: "Mr. Rockefeller wants the members to feel relaxed when the meeting is going on. He does not want them to be disrupted by reporters." Asked how the members intended to implement any decisions from the meeting, he said: "We are all important people. We can handle implementation all by ourselves."

A Phantom Trip

In his book about his press career in America, the British correspondent Louis Heren reminisced about the 1967 Arab-Israeli war. Tom Hughes, he said, had been dispatched to Gettysburg to see what he could find about the Eisenhower

Administration's alleged commitment to keep open the Gulf of Tiran. Since this story was completely spurious, TLH wrote to Heren complaining about his utterly false account and inquired about his source for this fabrication. In reply Heren wrote: "We are all getting older with memories beginning to fail. It was you yourself who told me of your Gettysburg trip." No further recourse.

★ ★ ★

A Phantom Career

When writing her 1998 book about Mary Pinchot Meyer, Nina Burleigh phoned TLH asking whether he might happen to have a photo of Mary taken when her husband, Cord, was the head of United World Federalists. TLH was able to unearth an attractive snapshot of Mary, taken at a world federalist meeting in Luxemburg in 1948, and he readily gave Burleigh permission to use it.

The book credited TLH for the photo, but the author's fertile imagination pressed on. She apparently assumed that there was something about the federalist movement that led all its leaders to join the CIA. She was right about Cord Meyer, but gratuitously erroneous when she stated on page 316 that "Tom Hughes also later joined the CIA." Thanks so much, Nina.

★ ★ ★

A Postwar Hamlet

In June, 1950, Michael Redgrave left postwar English rations and came to Denmark to star in Hamlet at Elsinore. TLH was in the audience when Redgrave suddenly forgot his lines and stumbled on stage. The announcer said the actor was temporarily indisposed from too much rich Danish food, and asked the audience to kindly tour the castle by torchlight until he recovered. We did and, in due course, he did.

★ ★ ★

Farewell to the Nantucket Grange

Jean Hughes was professionally interested in restoring antique properties. On Nantucket in the summer of 1970, she heard that the large, early 19th century, Grange meeting hall was about to be dismantled. The owner was the local bank, and she made inquiries. "Would you like it? We'll give it to you, if you will move it away. But you'll have to find a place on the island to put it." Jean and TLH spent the rest of their vacation unsuccessfully looking for an acceptable site. Ever since, they– and others–regretted their failure. The old building was soon demolished in favor of a parking lot.

★ ★ ★

Cosmos Club Lore

One afternoon in the mid-1950s, before TLH became a member and many years before women's membership became a lively issue, TLH was sitting in the lobby of the Cosmos Club in Washington while waiting to meet someone for lunch. A determined looking woman was knocking with her parasol at the front entrance on Massachusetts Avenue. The doorman admonished her, gently but firmly. "I'm sorry, madam, but ladies are not allowed to use the front entrance. You must go around the corner to the new ladies' entrance which we have just built for people like you."

"I'll just come through here," the woman retorted. "I am going upstairs to a meeting on Poland." "I'm sorry, madam, but only our members may use these doors. Please go around the corner to Florida Avenue, and come in properly at the ladies' entrance. "No," said the lady with the parasol. " I'll come in this way." Increasingly agitated, the attendant turned to TLH in desperation. "Madam, perhaps this fine young gentleman would be willing to escort you around to the ladies' entrance." Rising to the occasion, TLH soon found himself escorting Mrs. Woodrow Wilson, the same woman who, in 1919-20, had decided for the country "what was important and what was not."

Frolicking with the Argentine Ambassador

Late in life, a distinguished former White House aide, Chet Cooper, was a member of the history committee at the Cosmos Club. He was hot on the trail of archival material substantiating the rivalry, in the early 1920s, between Wallis Warfield and Mrs. Sumner Welles, then owner of the residence which the Cosmos today occupies. The Argentine ambassador in Washington was simultaneously enjoying the favors of both ladies. When the potential scandal was about to reach the press, Buenos Aires thought it best to recall the ambassador and avoid a diplomatic brouhaha. His removal from the Washington scene freed up Wallis Warfield to leave for England, where she first moved on to Mr. Simpson and then moved up to the Prince of Wales. Later Mr. Simpson was

quoted as saying that he regretted he had only one life to give
to his country and one wife to give to his king.

Mayor Barry's Success

At the height of the acrimony over women's admission to
membership, the Cosmos Club became the inadvertent
beneficiary of the otherwise undistinguished mayoralty of
Marion Barry. He threatened to take the liquor license away
from the all-male club if they continued to refuse to accept
women members. Under this threat, the most remarkable
transformation of attitude ensued. Once the choice was down
to admitting women or going dry, the transition to women's
membership suddenly became smooth.

The Cosmos Club's Shadow Cabinet

Since Washington, in the minds of many Cosmos members,
would be an obvious target for a nuclear attack, steps were
taken in 1994 to ensure its survival. To guarantee that the
club would rise as a phoenix from ground zero and a nuclear
nightmare, a shadow cabinet was organized out west with
members from the mountain states. A shadow president, vice
president, treasurer, et al, were designated. Since then, the
officers of the shadow cabinet have been ready to take over at a
moment's notice. But it has been almost two decades now, and
perhaps they are getting restive waiting to take office.

50 Calle San Francisco

After TLH and Jean fell in love with Old San Juan, they restored an old Spanish colonial house at 50 San Francisco Street. It was beautifully located just inside the Old San Juan gate and actually adjoined the police wing of the historic governor's mansion, La Fortaleza. While dealing with the Institute of Culture and its legendary director, Ricardo Alegría, they were told that they should talk to an old man who could be found, almost daily, sitting at the street corner next to Jewels of the World.

In the late 1960s, Jewels of the World was well known for its habit of dressing up its employees in police uniforms to escort tourists up from the docks directly to the store to do their shopping. Following the shoppers, TLH and Jean easily found the old man at the corner. They told him that they were restoring #50 San Francisco and his eyes lit up as he told his story.

In 1898 he had been a young lieutenant in the Royal Spanish artillery. He was summoned to El Morro to help defend the island against the imminent American invasion. "But when I reached the top of Christo Street, I paused. I saw the American ships on the horizon, and I asked myself whether I really wanted a career in the Spanish artillery. I quickly made the decision of a lifetime. The answer was no. So I proceeded down Christo to San Francisco Street and took refuge on the roof of the house that you are now restoring. I had a wonderful view of the American conquest, and I never regretted my decision."

Diplomatic Immunity

After TLH left the government, someone collided with his car on Massachusetts Avenue near the British embassy. A young policeman who witnessed the crash promptly came up to interrogate the parties. Casting an eye on the embassy. and worried about diplomatic immunity, he said: "No diplomats here, I hope." Once assured that no diplomats were involved, he then asked: "Anybody injured?" First things first.

Enduring Western Values

After World War II, a story circulated about the formidable commentator, Dorothy Thompson, who arrived one day in Tulsa, Oklahoma, to give a lecture. She was met at the train by an eager young student. He asked her what her topic would be that evening. She replied "The Decay of Western Values." His face fell. "Oh, Miss Thompson," he said, "Western values have only just come to Tulsa, Oklahoma."

On a related theme, Dave Barry more recently turned his attention to Miami, Florida. He described Miami as "a richly diverse cosmopolitan metropolis, where people from many different cultures live and work together while continuing to observe the traffic laws of their individual countries of origin."

Eternal Verities

When Chester Bowles, a Unitarian, visited Moscow in 1957, Ambassador Bohlen took him to visit an orthodox cathedral.

Aware that other visitors were crossing themselves as they entered the holy place, Bowles attempted a fumbling gesture. Bohlen cautioned him: "Please watch yourself, Chet. They fought wars here over whether you crossed yourself with three fingers or two."

TLH once attended a conference in Madeira. At the time, the local citizens were preoccupied with the Vatican's announced intention of starting the sainthood process for Emperor Karl, the last emperor of the Austro-Hungarian Empire, who had died in exile on the island. The local communist party was skeptical of his saintly qualifications and announced its opposition.

In its wisdom the municipal government decided to test matters by exhuming the dead emperor. When the onlookers, including the communists, saw the perfectly preserved body and uniform of the late emperor, all opposition evaporated. The communists agreed that anyone that well preserved must be a saint, withdrew their objection, and the beatification process resumed, unhindered by doubts.

Perhaps due to insufficient background vetting by his conservative clergy, Pope Benedict innocently appointed a new cardinal in Puerto Rico who turned out to be an Independentista. On his arrival at San Juan Cathedral, he reputedly removed the stars and stripes in the shrine to the Virgin Mary, leaving her draped, instead, entirely in the Puerto Rican flag.

The Second Coding

When in Jerusalem in 1950, TLH conversed with a rabbi whom he met in the lobby of the King David Hotel. The rabbi asked whether TLH was a Christian. Assurance was given that he was. The Israeli then told the story about a Christian priest who tried to convert a Jewish rabbi. The latter rebuffed conversion by saying:

"Look. You believe that the Messiah has already come, but also that he will come again. We believe that he has not yet come, but that he will. So we need not argue the point at all. When he comes we will ask him whether he was here before."

IX

FROM PILGRIMS TO

HOHENZOLLERNS
★ ★ ★

A New England Heritage

Probably inspired by the historian grandfather in whose house he grew up, TLH developed an early interest in family history. Both his grandmothers came from old New England families. Grandmother Hughes was a descendant of William and Susannah White who came over on the Mayflower. After William's death the first winter, Susannah married Edward Winslow, later Governor of Plymouth and the colony's first diplomat. Theirs was the first English marriage in New England.

The Whites' son, Peregrine, was actually born on the Mayflower while it was still anchored at Provincetown. He was thus the first English child born in New England. Later on, unfortunately, Peregrine ignored important Pilgrim strictures. He was convicted of fornication in his youth, and refrained from joining the church until very late in life.

★ ★ ★

The Windsor Churchyard

Both TLH and his first wife, Jean, were descended from
the much more upright Reverend Ephraim Huit, "teacher
in ye church at Windsor," who died in 1644. His celebrated
tombstone in the Windsor churchyard is the oldest one extant
in Connecticut. It carries the majestic lines:
"Who, when hee lived wee drew our vital breath
Who, when hee dyed his dying was our death.
Who was ye stay of state; ye church ye staff.
Alas, ye times forbid an epitaph!"

The Saga of Will Warren

In the late 1740s, Will Warren, another ancestor, was then
a youthful citizen of Farmington, Connecticut. He found
himself tormented by the "Great Awakening," then sweeping
the area. The religious fervor required church attendance twice
on Sunday, but Will preferred fishing with his Tunxis Indian
friends instead. The church fathers decided to punish this
insolence by putting Will in the stocks and pelting him with
rotten tomatoes after the Sunday morning service.

Will did not take this punishment lightly, and he retaliated
by starting to set fire to the great houses of Farmington. A
posse with dogs chased him around the surrounding hills until
his scent was lost. A town meeting concluded that Will had
been picked up by his warm-hearted Tunxis friends and carried
into Indian territory.

In 1771 Will, his Indian "wife", and their two children
were discovered by picnickers at the bottom of "Will

Warren's den" near Rattlesnake Mountain. Will's property was confiscated, but he was allowed to continue to live with his family in the den. His son Ahijah enlisted in the Revolutionary army and became a Congregational preacher in upstate New York.

A few decades later the skeletons of Will Warren and his spouse were discovered in the den. The Farmington town meeting then decided to give their bones to Miss Porter's School. For many years Will's skeleton was displayed for anatomical purposes on a pole in the Arts and Sciences building. Mrs. Warren's skull accompanied him in a hatbox. The fact that students at Miss Porter's, like Jackie Kennedy, may have learned anatomy by studying Will Warren still carries a certain charm.

Asked about Will's current whereabouts, a spokesman for the school told TLH "We know, but we are not at liberty to disclose." After proving his Warren descent, TLH also asked Indian officials in Connecticut whether he qualified for a cut from their casino proceeds. They claimed his connection was too remote.

★ ★ ★

The Battle of New Haven

Grandmother Lowe was a descendant of Ezra Stiles, the Revolutionary War president of Yale. Regarded as a Renaissance man in his day, he was unjustly deprived of the chance to become a famous strategist by the brevity of the British attack on New Haven. Stiles held himself in readiness to assume military command of Yale throughout the Revolution.

Stiles thought that the British would naturally raid Yale to capture such a conveniently assembled group of America's future leaders. So, in 1777, he dispersed the students to inland towns, accompanied by selected tutors—the freshmen to Farmington, the sophomores and juniors to Glastonbury, and the seniors to Wethersfield. A year later, finding himself more or less alone on campus, Stiles reassembled them at Yale, allowing volunteer students to "exhibit their sporting spirit" by fighting the British during vacations.

Taking the binoculars given to him by his friend Benjamin Franklin, Stiles regularly climbed up the steeple of the Congregational church in New Haven to look out to sea for the expected British ships.

On July 4, 1779, the British finally arrived. But instead of attacking Yale, they sauntered along East Wharf and burned a couple of small houses. After some minor skirmishes, they sailed away. Perplexed, and rather disappointed, Stiles sought an explanation. He began to leaf through the early Yale alumni lists, only to discover that the commander of one of the vessels in the British fleet was a graduate of the class of 1757.

Victims of their Times?

Edward Rawson was another early ancestor. He was the first secretary of the Massachusetts Bay Colony, and he signed the expulsion notices for unorthodox ministers who were "pernicious and heterodox in their doctrines." Another ancestor, Susannah Martin, despite her stout self-defense, was hanged for witchcraft at Salem.

Retrospectively Far-sighted

In 1853 TLH's great-grandmother Sybil Rawson Hills graduated at Oberlin, the first co-educational college in the country. Her future husband was a classmate, and together they were active in the Underground Railroad in Ohio, helping slaves escape from the south to freedom in the north. Another great-grandmother Sarah Smith Southwell was closely related to Sophia Smith, the founder of Smith College, and Mary Lyon, the founder of Mount Holyoke.

This same great-grandmother was a Civil War captain's widow. Sarah and her husband, Oran Southwell, had known Adlai Stevenson I in Illinois. In 1885, when Stevenson became Postmaster General in the first Cleveland administration, Sarah informed him of her then widowed circumstances, and she was granted a political appointment as postmistress of a small town in Minnesota. Since Cleveland had campaigned for Civil Service reform, Sarah was advised not to disclose her friendship for her Washington benefactor. When TLH told this story to Stevenson's grandson, Adlai II said: "They were politically prudent, even then."

20th Century Cousins

At the turn of the 20th century, political discussions in the Hughes family often involved their relatives. TLH's grandfather Hughes was a distant cousin of Charles Evan Hughes, who visited Mankato during his presidential campaign against Woodrow Wilson in 1916. Grandmother Hughes was related to President Grover Cleveland and

President William Howard Taft. Grandmother's sister had visited Washington during Cleveland's presidency. When she knocked on the front door of the White House, she was impressed when the President opened it himself.

A Carnegie Coincidence

Grandmother Hughes was also a distant cousin of Elihu Root, the Secretary of State and War under Theodore Roosevelt. Later Root managed to be a senator from New York at the same time that he served as the first president of the Carnegie Endowment (1910-25.) TLH followed him as the Endowment's fifth president a half century later (1971-91.)

Root was Andrew Carnegie's closest advisor. When asked in 1910 by Carnegie what it would cost to buy peace, Root quickly replied "$10,000,000." But Carnegie prudently worried about all contingencies, and wondered whether that amount would be either excessive or inadequate. He could easily afford a great deal more.

Root told him that if he insisted on second opinions, he should talk to his friends President Theodore Roosevelt in Washington and Kaiser Wilhelm in Berlin. Carnegie did so. He went to see Roosevelt, who thought that the whole concept of buying peace was absurd, but that $10 million was about right. Then Carnegie went to Europe and checked with the Kaiser. He agreed totally with Roosevelt—the idea was absurd, but $10 million was about right.

Root Also Advises TR

Elihu Root was as close an advisor to Theodore Roosevelt as he was to Andrew Carnegie. Although Root had been awarded the Nobel Prize for Peace in 1912, five years later, in February 1917, Root, TR, and Charles Evans Hughes—the then ranking Republican trio—met in New York and conspired to expedite hostilities. It was two months before America entered the war, but TR was eager to get into it ahead of time. He waxed eloquent about how he would volunteer to lead a regiment and would never come back. His sons would also go to France and they too would never return. Still President Wilson was refusing permission for them to go. Finally Root with his usual simple sagacity said: "Theodore, if you can convince Wilson that you will not come back, he will let you go."

All the Way with LBJ

Relatives in the next generation were more prosaic. One of them, however, unexpectedly turned up in Washington in 1965. Dr. George Hallenbeck of Minnesota's Mayo Clinic, was the chief surgeon for President Lyndon Johnson's famous kidney and gall bladder operation, the scars of which LBJ displayed to the press. The doctor's wife, Marian Mansfield, was a cousin of TLH's mother. After the operation, she was photographed wearing a Presidential gift, a pin that inevitably read "All the Way with LBJ."

Jean's Aunt Corinne

Another relative who colorfully flitted in and out of family life was Corinne Cameron, Jean's aunt. For many years she was the private secretary, first to Tallulah Bankhead, and then to Gertrude Lawrence. She was the source of much merriment in the Hughes household, including her line "a day away from Tallulah is like a month in the country."

TLH passed this quip along to Dean Rusk. He used it often in the late 1960s when temporarily freed from the ordeal of testifying on Vietnam before Fulbright and the Senate Foreign Relations Committee.

That ordeal also lay behind the decision in the State Department to present the Rusks with a silver tray when he retired as Secretary in 1969. It showed a stag and a doe eyeing one another in the forest, and the stag is saying: "Just remember, my dear, if we get through this weekend, we'll be out of season."

Prohibition and Bohemian Grove

German Ambassador Werner Otto von Hentig was another distant cousin. He became famous as the Teutonic version of Lawrence of Arabia. He had led the German mission to Afghanistan in World War I, in an effort to proclaim India a republic and to stimulate a revolt there against British rule. (TLH wrote up this colorful episode in the German Studies Review, October, 2002.)

Von Hentig was appointed German consul-general in San Francisco in the 1920s. One of his friends there was another would-be war-hero, the later General Douglas MacArthur, who was then commandant at the Presidio. Prohibition was still the law of the land, and MacArthur's thirsty garrisons needed a reliable supplier of wines and liquor. Hentig rose to the occasion, and once a week MacArthur sent a Presidio truck to the German Consulate to collect the necessary, diplomatically boot-legged, supplies. In addition to his regular reimbursements, MacArthur invited von Hentig to be his guest at the all-male festivities at Bohemian Grove.

A War Not a Treaty

Von Hentig's sister was married to Ernst Eisenlohr, the German minister in Prague during the Munich crisis in 1938. Like his brother- in-law, he was a professional foreign service officer and anti-Nazi. In an effort to stave off the invasion that he saw coming, Eisenlohr took the initiative in privately negotiating a draft treaty with the Czech government to avert the coming catastrophe.

Eisenlohr took his draft treaty to Berlin and gave it to Foreign Minister von Ribbentrop, saying that the treaty was acceptable to the Czechs and was a way to avoid war. Ribbentrop replied: "You horse's ass. We want a war, not a treaty." Eisenlohr quickly resigned from the foreign service, and sat out the war in Badenweiler, where the postwar French occupiers appointed him mayor.

A Hohenzollern Connection

TLH is only 1/16th German, but his relationship with the former German royal family has been one of the more exotic aspects of his private life. It began in 1938 with his discovery that his German great-great grandfather, Charles Frederick Schlaberg (1794-1883) was a lineal descendant in the male line from the early 16th century Hohenzollern electors of Brandenburg. Like his father, Schlaberg had been named Charles Frederick for his distant cousin, King Frederick the Great of Prussia.

In 1812 at age 18, Schlaberg left French-occupied Hildesheim to avoid conscription in the French army for Napoleon's invasion of Russia. After fifteen years in Edinburgh and fifty years in Quebec, Schlaberg moved to Minneapolis in his old age. During his lifetime he began the family collection of Hohenzollern-related porcelains, bronzes, sculpture, portraits, ancient books, maps, and coins. Over the generations some 300 letters from Hohenzollerns in Germany were also saved. During two world wars, of course, these German items had been consigned to the attic. Schlaberg's male descendants were all loyal Americans who enlisted to fight Germany in both conflicts. Many of them were probably unaware of their German connection.

Reconnecting with Royal Relatives

TLH, however, was undeterred. When he was 13 and 14, he wrote and typed up a two volume history of the Hohenzollern family. The exiled Kaiser Wilhelm II sent him autographed photos annually on his birthday, and the Kaiser's widow wrote letters both before and after World War II. TLH also corresponded with all five of the Kaiser's surviving sons and, over the succeeding decades, he knew five of the grandsons and several of the great-grandchildren. Some of them visited TLH in Washington. His personal conversations and extensive correspondence with the family have been written up elsewhere.

The English Branch

One of the Kaiser's grandsons, Prince Frederick of Prussia, was at Cambridge when World War II broke out. He was a godson of King George V and was protected by the British royal family. During the war he commanded the so-called Pioneer Brigade of anti-Nazi Germans who worked in Canada. TLH corresponded with him there. By the time TLH arrived at Oxford in 1947, Frederick, then known locally as "Mr. Mansfield," had married into the Guinness family and lived a rural life in Little Haddam, Hertfordshire. In 1948 TLH visited him and his wife there and in their London apartment as well. One of their daughters eventually married the future Duke of Wellington.

A Hohenzollern and a Wittelsbach

In Munich in 1950, TLH was walking around a newly restored part of he old town with Prince Burchard of Prussia, another of the Kaiser's grandsons. They were discussing the

Bavarian royal family, the Wittelsbachs. Suddenly Burchard said: "I spy a Wittelsbach right now, right over there. Come and meet him." After they greeted one another, Burchard went on to say: "People always accuse us of introducing insanity into the Bavarian royal family. But look at him. He's perfectly normal."

In the Former German Colonies

Burchard was a lawyer with the Munich Reinsurance Company. He frequently visited Africa, and occasionally a black German-African group in Togo or Cameroon would assemble in his honor. Old Prussian helmets, imperial uniforms, and military decorations would reappear for the occasion. "One by one a group of heel- clicking black men would then introduce themselves with famous old Prussian names like "Graf Kraft von Delmingsingen or Graf Otto von Alvensleben,"

A Hohenzollern Shade at the Plimptons'

As a wedding present before the first World War, the Kaiser gave his second son, Prince Eitel Friedrich, the handsome Italian Renaissance Villa Balbianello, located on the southwest shore of Lake Como. Upon Italy's entry into the war, it was confiscated as enemy property. That was the last that the prince saw of it.

An AEF veteran from the Ames family of Massachusetts lingered in the area after the armistice, and he eventually bought the villa from the Italian government. He arranged for members of the larger Ames family to vacation there, a few weeks each year. Mrs. Francis Plimpton was one of them. Her husband, a prominent New York lawyer, was deputy to Adlai Stevenson at the UN in the Kennedy administration. The Plimptons' friends, and those of their well-known son George, vacationed there frequently. TLH and Jean were among them, but, in addition, they also had a link to Balbianello's Hohenzollern past.

★ ★ ★

"Texas Willy"

When the then head of the Hohenzollern family, Prince Louis Ferdinand of Prussia, arrived in Washington in October 1956, he had been visiting his sister in Texas. During World War II LF had been closely involved in the ill-fated anti-Hitler conspiracy. A friend and guest of Franklin Roosevelt before the war, he considered himself a "New Deal Democrat." He was also a postwar friend of Willy Brandt, the youthful mayor of West Berlin, and he had just persuaded Democratic Governor Shivers to appoint Brandt an honorary colonel in Texas.

★ ★ ★

The Kaiser's Influentials

One of TLH's Oxford friends, Bill Emerson, became the director of the Roosevelt library at Hyde Park, New York. He located a file of Prince Louis Ferdinand's personal correspondence with FDR, and TLH took it to LF in Germany to replace copies that had been lost in the war.

In passing, Emerson asked whether the Kaiser's childhood friend, Poultney Bigelow, was correct in claiming that he was responsible for the ex-monarch's taking up wood chopping in his Dutch exile. TLH put the question to Louis Ferdinand, and he replied: "Please tell Professor Emerson that it is such a good story that it would be a shame to discredit it. Let's just assume that Bigelow was right."

The prince went on to say that he could authoritatively verify the influence that Andrew Carnegie also had on Wilhelm II. His grandfather had told him that Carnegie had inspired him to create the Kaiser Wilhelm Institutes (now the Max Planck Institutes) which have played such an important role in intellectual and scientific circles in Europe.

Lili Damita

In the mid-1920s Louis Ferdinand had had an intimate Hollywood relationship with the French actress, Lili Damita, later the wife of Errol Flynn. LF was amused that Jack Kennedy claimed to have enjoyed the same privileges from "Tiger Lili" at the Arizona Biltmore in 1945. TLH told the prince that JFK had taken the old maxim "to err is human, to forgive divine" and reformulated it: "To Errol is human, to Flynn divine."

"Uncle Niehans"

The German postwar tabloids, then as now, dealt mostly in sex and royal scandals. In 1956 they were featuring LF's "Uncle Niehans." Dr. Paul Niehans of Switzerland had become famous all over Europe for his rejuvenating shots of calf-embryo serum. LF said that Adenauer and the Pope had benefitted regularly from the Niehans treatment.

The tabloids also alleged that Niehans was an illegitimate grandson of Kaiser Friedrich III. LF agreed that "Niehans looks more and more like a Hohenzollern, the older he gets. He resembles my Uncle Oskar very much." Niehans himelf was embarrassed by the articles, and asked LF if he could intervene with the publishers to get them to stop. LF laughed and told him that he was delighted with the alleged relationship, "and besides, as far as I know, everything they say is perfectly true. If you don't mind, we don't."

A Chance Meeting in the Senate

In 1956 TLH took Prince Louis Ferdinand to lunch in the US Senate Restaurant. Senator Key Pittman had given him bourbon on his last visit there, during LF's honeymoon in 1938. The prince was a railway buff, and he was particularly delighted with the small Senate subway. As he took his seat in the little railway car, who should be sitting opposite but Woodrow Wilson's grandson, Dean Francis Sayre of the Washington Cathedral. TLH introduced him to the Kaiser's grandson and both proclaimed their encounter to be "poignant and memorable."

Anglo-German Postwar Niceties

When Queen Elizabeth visited Germany in 1965, she was entertained at an elaborate state dinner to which Prince Louis

Ferdinand was invited. The host was West German President Heinrich Luebke. He was a farmer who had risen in the Christian Democratic party and was the first German head of state to host a British royal figure in five decades.

According to LF, when the time for toasts arrived, Luebke rose and said: "Vat a vonderful occasion this is, indeed. I now ask you all to be up-standing and join with me in the famous old toast, "Upon the Queen!" (Presumably this was a rough rendition in English of "an die Koenigin," which could mean "to" but also means "upon.")

★ ★ ★

Joachim's Suit of Armor

During the Prussian Exhibition in Berlin in 1980, TLH was a guest of Prince Louis Ferdinand at a recital of his "Lieder," sung by Edda Moser, the well known opera soprano. They all had dinner at the prince's Berlin residence on Koenigstrasse in Dahlem in a party that included the soloist and the director of the exhibition. The exhibits on the premises included the 16th century suit of armor that had once belonged to TLH's and LF's common ancestor, Elector Joachim II of Brandenburg. Both agreed that they would have to shrink a good deal to fit inside.

★ ★ ★

Ancestral Castles

On more than one occasion, TLH and his sons, Evan and Allan, have visited the spectacular Hohenzollern castle in Hechingen as guests of the family. Located in southern

Germany in the Swabian Alps, this "Stammsitz" was the ancient Hohenzollern residence dating from the 11th century. Equally fascinating have been visits to the Jagellonian palace in Cracow, Poland. There the cathedral and reception rooms can still be seen where, in 1535, Joachim II, elector of Brandenburg, married Hedwig, the eldest daughter of King Sigismund I of Poland. Their son was TLH's ancestor, Archbishop Sigismund of Magdeburg (1538-66.) Before his death from the plague at age 28, the young archbishop, the eldest grandson of King Sigismund I, was a promising candidate for the Polish throne.

The Archivo Secreto

Once when in Rome, TLH arranged an appointment at the Vatican to see what, if anything, their archives contained concerning Archbishop Sigismund's short life. TLH was alone with the attendant and his files, except for some monks peering down at them from a balcony above. "To what do I owe this cloud of witnesses?" TLH asked. "Because you are an ab initio reader." "You mean the first reader this week?" "No, the first reader ever." The Sigismund papers had remained unopened since 1566.

Out of the dusty file tumbled the 1553 parchment letter from Emperor Charles V to the College of Cardinals, recommending young Sigismund's appointment as archbishop. "It's true that he is only 14, but his tutor will accompany him and his father, after all, reigns in Berlin." By 1562 the 24-year-old-archbishop's reputation was highly positive at the Vatican, except for reports that he had moved Anna Schlaberg, his mistress, into the archbishop's palace in Halle, where they were living with their two small children.

Pope Pius IV summarized the situation in a letter to the young archbishop: "Dear Brother in Christ: We hear nothing but the highest praise for your ecclesiastical accomplishments in Magdeburg. Your visits to the monasteries are especially commendable...There's just this one thing. We are confident that, when the truth reaches the Holy See, the malicious rumors that have come to our attention can be put aside." Following this gentle papal admonition, Sigismund moved his girlfriend and the children out of the residence to the Gruener Hof, a new home he bought for them a mile away. For a few years it was a happy arrangement for all concerned. Anna survived, lived to a great age, and was a beloved lady bountiful in the area.

A Donation to Yale

After the death of Prince Louis Ferdinand, the Hohenzollern succession went to his charming young grandson, Prince George Frederick. In 2008 GF visited the Hugheses in Chevy Chase and they went over the large Schlaberg-Hohenzollern collection. Although GF would have liked parts of it for the family castle in Hechingen, he understood TLH's preference to keep the entire collection intact and in the United States, if the right depository institution could be found.

Yale University soon decided it wanted the collection in toto. So in 2010-11 hundreds of letters, books, maps, portraits, engravings, porcelains, bronzes, ceramics, and coins were donated to Yale where they can now be found at the Beinecke

Museum for Rare Books and Manuscripts, the Sterling Library, the Yale Art Gallery, and the Yale Center for British Art.

Going away parties for the collection were held in Washington and were attended by two members of the German royal family who now live in the U.S. A couple of amusing ironies were involved in the donation to Yale. The music for Yale university's official anthem, "Bright College Years," turns out to have been lifted directly in the late 19th century from the German national anthem of imperial Hohenzollern days, "The Watch on the Rhine."

Also, by coincidence, the president of the New York firm that appraised the collection was Elizabeth von Habsburg. When TLH mentioned that he was aware of certain historical Hohenzollern-Habsburg difficulties, like the wars of 1740 and 1866, she assured him that history would not adversely affect the objectivity of her appraisal. "Let's consider it a nice kind of closure."

In 2011 on the day when the last shipment left Chevy Chase for New Haven, the Washington good music station, WGMS, also cooperated by playing Bach's Brandenburg concertos as the objects went out the door.

★ ★ ★

A 2011 Royal Wedding

At the end of August 2011, TLH and his wife Jane attended the wedding festivities in Germany of Prince George Frederick to Princess Sophia of Isenburg. On opening night, a gala concert was held in Berlin for a thousand guests including many of the has-beens of Europe. The Romanovs, Bourbons,

Habsburgs, and Gonzagas were all represented. The next day 450 invitees in wedding finery took off for the wedding itself, which was held in the Friedenskirche (Peace Church) in the Sans Souci complex at Potsdam.

The entire event was televised. Jane and TLH later learned that, while walking to the church, they had suddenly appeared on the screen—TLH in "dunkler Anzug" (formal dark suit) and Jane in a green silk suit with matching shoes and handbag, and a splendid hat with a green satin ribbon and jade brooch. A TV observer in Munich said of Jane: "Now there is an elegant lady."

★ ★ ★

The Mystery Couple

One of the journalists lining the route asked the TV historian-genealogist who these Americans were. He shuffled through his papers before the camera, confessing that "at the moment, I don't really know." When they were leaving the church the cameraman put them on TV once more, and the same expert said, "Mein Gott, it's the mystery couple again!"

The groom's secretary was in charge of transport from the church to the Neue Kammern, an 18th century San Souci reception residence built by Frederick the Great. Gesturing toward the assembled Mercedes and Bentleys, she announced in a loud voice: "Imperial Highnesses! This way, PLEASE!" This separated the imperial guests like the Romanovs and the Habsburgs from those of mere royal rank, like the Saxons and the Bavarians.

Drinks in the garden preceded the elegant formal reception in the palace. When ultimately ushered in for their private minutes with the bridal couple, Jane was able to display a charming picture on her iPhone of the groom sitting in the Hughes living room when he had visited them in Chevy Chase three years earlier.

★ ★ ★

Macmillan Speaks for Balliol

In his old age, former Prime Minister Harold Macmillan, a prominent Balliol College, Oxford, alumnus, came to the Wilson Center in Washington. Some hundred guests were eager to hear his remarks after dinner. He was seated on a little dais, resting on his cane, and looking very sleepy. Some in the audience were afraid that he was in danger of something worse. Jim Billington, another Oxonian, presided. He opened the proceedings by saying, "I see Tom Hughes is here. Like the Prime Minister, he's an old Balliol man. I'm sure he has a question." MacMillan remained imperturbable.

TLH rose and said in a loud voice: "Prime Minister, I have just been reading a biography of Kaiser Wilhelm II. It seems that his grandmother, Queen Victoria, wanted him to go to Balliol in the 1870s. But Bismarck thought that Balliol was unsuitable for a Prussian prince, and he vetoed the proposal. Question: what would have happened if the Kaiser had gone to Balliol?"

Macmillan did not stir. There was growing apprehension in the audience. Following a prolonged silence, the hand on the cane moved slightly. Gradually one eye opened. Then the other. Suddenly the old man became fully alert, and he responded in a firm voice: "He would have won the war."

Envoi: Silence is Preferred

In the 1920s, an English aristocrat, Daisy, Princess of Pless, wrote some popular autobiographies. The titles of her last two books were: "Better Left Unsaid" and "What I left Unsaid." Perhaps TLH should have been cautioned by Daisy's experience when he lunched at the Garrick Club one noon in the 1980s. The Garrick is where the London actors and spies commingle. The discrete sign on the common table proclaimed the rules clearly enough: "Silence is Preferred."

TLH obediently ate his main course in silence, sitting opposite a man who looked vaguely familiar. But as dessert was being served, TLH's brash American instincts took over. Deliberately turning the silence card upside down, he ventured to address the member opposite. "If you will pardon my saying so, sir, you bear a strong resemblance to the family attorney in 'Upstairs, Downstairs'." He responded: "Yes, I am he, but you would never know it from the ridiculous royalties that I get from your country." With that, he returned the "Silence Is Preferred" card to its proper upright position.

By now, patient reader, you probably agree.

26134283R10167

Made in the USA
Charleston, SC
25 January 2014